The Missing Piece in Self-Love

Love Yourself from the Inside Out

Compiled By Kate Gardner

The Missing Piece in Self-Love, Love Yourself from the Inside Out:

Copyright © 2015 by Kate Gardner

www.themissingpieceinbouncingback.com

All right reserved. Printed in the United States of American & the UK. No part of this book may be used or reproduced in any manner whatsoever without written permission except in the case of brief quotations em- bodied in critical articles or reviews.

Although the authors and publisher have made every effort to ensure that the information in this book was correct at press time, the author and publisher do not assume and hereby disclaim any liability to any party due to these words coming from the authors own "Personal Opinion" of their experiences.

Every word in this book is based on the authors own personal experience of own personal development journey, and the outcomes of clients that they may have witnessed.

Although we have made every reasonable attempt to achieve complete accuracy in the content of this book, we assume no responsibility for errors or omissions if the information in this book happens to be carried out by yourself.

You should only use this information as you see fit at your own risk. Your life and circumstances may not be suited to these examples with what we share amongst these pages.

The authors and publisher are neither a doctor or in a position of registered authority to give you expert advice. All we can share is what we have tested on ourselves and obtained through witnessing the changes in our lives or our clients lives along the way.

How you choose to include this information in this book within your own life is completely your own responsibility and own risk.

The Missing Piece Publishing House

Seathorne Walk

Bridlington

East Yorkshire, YO16 7QP

England

For information visit www.themissingpiecepublishing.com

Book and Cover Design by Jennifer Insignares

www.yourdesignsbyjen.com

ISBN: 978-1-51360-186-1

Table of Contents

Introduction 1

Chapter 1: Feeding or Fighting
By Angela Mosley 6

Chapter 2: From Madness to Mindfulness
By Claire Hartman-James 13

Chapter 3: Garfield and Nineteen Days
By Debbie McLaren 20

Chapter 4: The Game Changer
By Donna Porteous 26

Chapter 5: Loving Her to the Bones
By Ellis Panda 32

Chapter 6: Self-Love – My Awakening, My Salvation
By Freyja P. Jensen 39

Chapter 7: You Are a Miracle
By Greg Fletcher 45

Chapter 8: From Rock Bottom to Self-love
By Jennifer Insignares 52

Chapter 9: A Woman, Rising
By Kirsty Holland 58

Chapter 10: My Journey to Self-Love
By Laurie Reid 65

Chapter 11: You're Perfectly Human
By Leigh Burton 71

Chapter 12: Beautifully Broken
By Letisha Galloway 78

Chapter 13: What's Love Got to Do With It?
By Lisa Beane 85

Chapter 14: Self-Love: The Art of Acceptance
By Lori Blake-Leighton 92

Chapter 15: From Brokenness to Wholeness
By Lynn Jones 98

Chapter 16: From Breakdown Comes Breakthrough
By Matthew Cipes 104

Chapter 17: Who Am I?
By Maxine Browne 110

Chapter 18: Lead By a Whisper
By Meghan Yates 117

Chapter 19: Beauty and the Beast
By Mofoluwaso Ilevbare 125

Chapter 20: From Slopes to Syringes to Serenity
By Nathaniel J. Grigsby 131

Chapter 21: Digging In
By Pam Robertson 138

Chapter 22: My Journey from Hating to Accepting and Loving Myself
By Patricia LeBlanc RM(T) 145

Chapter 23: Ear of the Beholder
By Richelle Traversano 152

Chapter 24: Look Around You
By Shannon Hrobak Sennefelder 158

Chapter 25: We Must Not Only Educate the Mind, But Also the Heart
By Sylvia Friedman 165

Chapter 26: Self-Love – Selflessly Selfish
By Toni Idiaquez 172

Chapter 27: Filling Up on God's Love
By Violeta Rajacic 178

Chapter 28: Unravelling Your Real Self
By Virin Gomber 185

Chapter 29: The "Lost Puppy" Syndrome
By Yvette Mason.. 192

Conclusion... 198

Compiled By Kate Gardner

Introduction

Self-love is something that almost every person on this planet struggles with at some point in their lives. Only it's sad that in order to get to that point of self-love we first have to self-hate, and am not just talking about not liking ourselves. I am talking about hating ourselves so much that we refuse to even look in a mirror. I know! I did this myself in my late 20's and the mirrors in my house gradually got reduced to the point where I only had a little cabinet hung in my bathroom where I could just see my head and shoulders reflecting back at me.

It was not long after the births of my children that I hated what had happen to my once slim figure. That plus a mental torturing affair with my boss at the time, had completely stripped me of my self-confidence. At the time you don't notice that you hate yourself, in fact it starts to become a habit and, unless you're highly self-aware of your actions, then you will continue to go on a downward spiral. It will start with you calling yourself "stupid", or you will say things like "Why can't I ever do anything right?"… I know you are reading this right now and can completely get with what am saying because we have all done this at some stage!

So, while we are making these statements to our sub conscious minds every single day, we then make them into beliefs and start acting upon them beliefs, just like I did, and I started removing mirrors from my home and hiding under black baggy clothes. I stopped wearing make-up and could no longer be bothered to make myself look presentable. I actually got to the point where I was so depressed I wanted to kill myself, because I thought "Who would miss me?"

The Missing Piece in Self-Love

I would hate having my photo taken and would hide right at the back of a crowd when there was a group photo. I wanted to fade into the background and not be seen because being centre stage would mean I would have to see myself on a photo and hate what I was staring back at even more when I viewed the photo. Crazy to hear these statements from somebody who is now highly visible online and a public figure and places herself in front of thousands and thousands of people every day, right?

That is because after a long hard journey, I learnt what it took to really place yourself first and gain high self-respect and love for yourself. It was one bitch of a roller coaster ride to get to this point of where I am today! However it was so worth it!

Learning to love myself was a baby-step process, and with a bit of work each day I stepped closer to my main aim of rising my self-love levels. Even now to the point where I love being in front of the camera.

What I did learn from my journey is that unless I loved myself at a high vibration, there was no way I could love those around me at the levels they deserved. So the more I fell in love with me, then the more I fell in love with those around me. Which in return made me a better mother, partner, friend, CEO, and coach to my clients. Every subject that I compile in **The Missing Piece Book Series** is always close to my heart. This book is just the same! I wanted to bring forward many amazing stories from 29 amazing authors to provide hope on your journey, and to let you know that the journey from self-hate to self-love is something that 95% of the world goes through on a daily basis.

I hope by sharing the authors' stories with you in this powerful book that it gives you hope and amazing steps that you can place into your own self-love journey. You deserve to look in the mirror (a big bloody tall mirror) each day and love what stares back at

Compiled By Kate Gardner

you! You are beautiful, you are amazing, and you deserve to shine brighter than any star in the sky.

It's a complete honour to compile this book and bring to you a subject so powerful, and to bring hope to those, who like myself many years ago, didn't see how truly beautiful and amazing they really are. I proudly present to you 29 amazing authors in '**The Missing Piece in Self-Love; Love Yourself from the Inside Out.**'

I never get tired of placing hope into the world with these books!

Much Love & Appreciation

Kate Gardner

9 x Best-Selling Author/Speaker/Coach &

CEO of The Missing Piece Publishing House

www.themissingpiecepublishing.com

www.kate-gardner.co.uk

The Missing Piece in Self-Love

Angela Mosley

Angela Mosley is an Author as well as an Intuitive Editor and Ghost-writer for the thought leaders and transformational coaches of today.

As an Editor, Angela helps her clients communicate their written message with more power and clarity. When ghost-writing, Angela harnesses her client's unique voice and speaking mannerisms and translates them into a powerful written project.

Angela believes that every person has a unique story to tell and that every story needs to be told. Her passion is to help people translate the passion of their hearts and messages into words that come to life on a page.

You can reach Angela at:

Website:
www.angelamosley.com

Email:
angela@angelamosley.com

Facebook:
AngelaMosleyEditor

Compiled By Kate Gardner

Twitter:
@angelamosley

Feeding or Fighting

By Angela Mosley

Nobody wants to feel depressed. Yet, for more than half of my life, that is the identity that I wore: major depression, with recurrent episodes. I grew up in a dysfunctional home, and that experience left many scars and emotional issues that I've had to work through. I went through various forms of psychotherapy over the course of five years and through trial and error found an antidepressant medication that seemed to work best for me. Yet, despite all the years of therapy and the daily medication, I still felt the shades of depression around me, and I couldn't figure out why. I knew, deep inside (though I never said it out loud), that I had the ability to somehow not be depressed, as if I knew what to do to cure my depression. I couldn't put my finger on what this was, exactly, though. So I just continued to take my medication and visit a therapist for regular mental check-ups.

Because my heart would not stop its whisperings of *"You know the answer to this puzzle….you know what your 'cure' is…"* I began a journey of honest self-discovery. I started asking God and myself hard questions like *"If everything that happens to us is meant to lead us closer to our complete purpose, what is my purpose? Help me to understand, not all the little reasons why every event that shaped me happened the way it did, but help me to understand why my life has happened FOR me this way. What is MY truth? What are MY unique gifts that I'm meant to bring to the world?"*

When you honestly start to ask those questions, you get answers.

Compiled By Kate Gardner

One day in the summer of 2014, I saw myself very clearly in my mind's eye. What I saw was simply ME: my mind, my gifts, and my own thoughts, uncolored by outside perceptions. Then I saw an actual shadow of me, separate from my body, and stand facing me. This shadow was gray, head bowed, eyes downcast, shoulders slumped. I knew right away that this shadow was Depression. In my mind's eye, I stared in amazement at this Shade. I realized, with absolute certainty (for the first time in my life), "That is not who I AM. That is separate from me, and I can choose to take her hand and walk with her. Or I can choose to walk away." In that moment, I felt such compassion for this Shade, burdened with years of pain and doubt and fear that had never been allowed to heal. I stood before her, marvelling at her complexity, for she carried swirls of sadness from so many people whom I care I so much about. Her sadness was beautiful, but tragic, because I knew I would never be able to understand her completely, or help her to be happy. She existed, and she was real. But I knew she was no longer a part of me *unless I wanted her to be. She didn't belong to me—**and she never had.***

In that moment, I began to cry tears of sadness for all that the Shade carried, and tears of happiness for the realization that all those burdens were never authentically mine. I actually cried out, "That's not mine! That isn't me! Freedom—I am FREE to choose!"

Until that moment, I had never considered that I had the traits of an empath. Yet as I processed all my life experiences and feelings and as more intuitive visions and empathic connections came to me, I began to understand that I am highly intuitive and empathic. As an intuitive adolescent and young adult, I had read the thoughts and emotions of those around me. As an empath, I had reached out to help carry some of those thoughts and emotions. Except….I never put them down when the time to carry them was over.

The Missing Piece in Self-Love

When I finally realized that the depression and negativity were not mine to carry, I felt such relief. Then, as I began to see these traits of empathy and intuition rising up within me, I became angry. Why do I have this gift that causes me so much pain? Why do I have to feel what others feel? Know what others are thinking? Know what's going to happen before it happens? I wanted to fight it. I wanted to turn it off. I wanted to not "feel" this way.

Then, these words came to me: *Feed what you love, instead of fighting what you hate.*

I thought at first that the words were meant for my physical health because I was also trying to make some health changes around this time. So, I interpreted the message to mean: Instead of fighting the sugar cravings, try feeding your body healthy foods to make it feel better. That's good advice, right? So, I started to do that. I started making healthier choices physically, but emotionally and mentally I was feeling frustrated and discouraged that the intuitive empathic side of me wanted to come through. I kept hearing *Feed, Don't Fight,* stronger and more clearly. I was missing the point somewhere.

One day it clicked that the message was meant for more than just my physical world. It was meant for my emotional and mental world. I began, begrudgingly at first, to accept the intuitive and empathic parts of myself. I began looking at my intuition as a gift that helped me understand people. I tried to see my empathy as a gift that helped me help others when they needed it. I had no idea, however, how to feed these aspects of my identity. (Honestly, I wasn't sure I wanted to, but I knew I had to.) So, I did what I always do when I need information: I turned to books.

I learned that intuitive and empathic people need things like calm, quiet time in nature, different types of meditations, longer showers or baths with specific essential oils to calm the mental and emotional noise, and even more sleep than most people, because this type of connection to the world around us can be so draining. Instead of fighting the intuitive and empathic pieces of myself, I began to feed them what they needed. I was curious to see what would happen to them if I fed them, and I also knew that continuing to ignore them was beginning to negatively impact my physical health.

I made a promise to myself to honor every intuitive message that I received. Once I made that promise, I began to receive more and more intuitive messages. Each time I fed that part of me by speaking or acting on the message I had received, I would receive another message. Honestly, I'm still learning how to feed the empathic part of myself. This process is a challenge for me, because of my introverted nature. But I have found that when I acknowledge what I am feeling as being someone else's energy and not my own, I can take steps to help the other person through that emotion or take steps to clear myself of that energy if there is nothing I can do to help the other person.

As I think more about this idea of feeding what I love instead of fighting what I hate, I realize that it's a daily question I have to ask myself, "*Will this nourish my heart, mind, soul, or body?*" If the answer is no, then I have to make a choice to walk away or to do it anyway (knowing that I am not showing my Self any love when I do it). This is not an easy truth to wrestle with. Everything that does not feed life into me contributes in some way to a form of death. At the same time, there is a tremendous sense of freedom and power in embracing the truth of feeding or fighting. When I focus more on feeding what I love, the things I hate seem to fade into the background, and I begin to honestly love the Self that I see.

The Missing Piece in Self-Love

Please Note: *I do not mean to say that all depression is the outcry of an unrecognized intuitive or empathic spirit, nor do I intend to say that depression is easy to walk away from. If you are trying to live through depression, please seek out a compassionate and educated network of people who can help you address all the facets of this complicated issue. Periods of my depression were intense and nearly took my life. I will always carry the intensity of those experiences with me. I share this side of my story with you with the hope that it may encourage you to look at every aspect of yourself with compassion and love. Focus on feeding the parts you love, and you just might find—as I did—that the parts you hate start to diminish more easily.*

Compiled By Kate Gardner

Claire Hartman-James

Claire Hartman-James is a successful online brand, six figure entrepreneur and personal development coach. Her married name is Hartman and her maiden name is James, the two merged in a simple online error to form a brand name.

Her main purpose and passion is in sharing her story of going from broke mentally, emotionally and financially, to living a happy (almost fulfilled life) in order to inspire others to take action for change. Claire offers unconditional love and support, to encourage ordinary people to explore the full potential they hold within, this is the key to unleashing their extraordinary power...

Using her vast self-taught knowledge and personal experience of using the law of attraction, and the power of the positive mind, Claire motivates others to success, leading by example. Her current business has enabled her the financial freedom to further explore her passions in this area.

Claire's overall vision is to spread awareness of postnatal psychosis and the way we can improve our mental state of health and well-being naturally. This is rare condition that effects approximately 1 in 1000 women during the postnatal period. Claire was hospitalised nearly 9 years ago, 3 weeks after the birth of her son Bayley. She suffered extreme panic attacks, paranoia, delusions, sleep paralysis, nightmares and hallucinations. Not knowing the difference between day and night, hot or cold, and even having a 'secret code' to trust she was speaking to her own husband. Claire and her family faced an extremely scary time with a new born baby and only four months later she lost her twin sister to drink, drugs and depression.

Claire spent the next year recovering and made a brave decision after 3 weeks on anti-psychotic drugs to cope naturally by facing her fears rather than masking with medication. Although this is not something she recommends, she teaches others through video and social media, how to cope with the many obstacles life throws at us, to look for the good in any given situation, however tough it may feel at the time.

Featuring in this book and future books is a stepping stone in the direction of her vision. Her ultimate goal is to write her own books and speak on stage, offering love, light, and inspiration to many.

You can reach Claire at:

Email:
Claire.positiveminds@gmail.com

Website:
www.workwithclaire.com

Blog:
www.clairehartman.com

Facebook:
www.facebook.com/cairehartman

Compiled By Kate Gardner

From Madness to Mindfulness: The Tough Lessons in Self-Love
By Claire Hartman-James

'Please Put On Your Own Oxygen Mask Before Assisting Others'

Pretty crazy eh? When our natural instinct is to put our own children first...however, the only way to ensure that you can truly help those around you is to help yourself first, therefore the instruction from the flight attendant to "put on your own oxygen mask before helping those around you" is very relevant.

Self-love is a toughie for most of us, yes we can be selfish at times, or a complete martyr at others, however, how many of us really truly practice or know what self-love really is?

Let me tell you my story of how I learnt my lesson the hard way...

Growing up as one of three girls, a twin, yet the middle one, I always found that by standing up for and putting myself first, I didn't get walked over so much. As a teen and young twenty something, I wasn't the easiest person to please. I wouldn't stand any nonsense, so it was normally my way or the high way. I could pretty much cope with anything and had zero tolerance for weakness or people taking advantage of me. I was a strong minded young lady. Both my sisters married their first loves; Penny, my twin, after falling pregnant at 16... whilst I, on the other hand, went from one relationship to another, pushing them to their limits. Then, in my early twenties, I married my RAF Sergeant for completely the wrong reasons. I knew he was no good, I knew he drank too much, I knew he was possessive and

The Missing Piece in Self-Love

I knew he would try to control me. I also knew he had been married twice already, and had a disastrous track record. My Mum and my Auntie even questioned my love for him beforehand, yet I was adamant I would prove them all wrong.

I was secretly desperate to go to Holland. He was getting posted there, it made perfect sense to me to get married, leave the RAF and see more of the world. I could handle the rest I'm sure. Holland was great, the people amazing, however, the marriage not so...

After a short, yet violent, emotional rollercoaster, ending in him publicly humiliating me at a friend's wedding, I walked away with nothing and returned to England with my tail between my legs to start again.

Eventually, after several more failed relationship attempts, when I wasn't looking, I found my soul mate. It was literally 'eyes across the room', 'love at first sight'. Everything felt right, he didn't want or try to change me and accepted me fully, despite my many flaws. You could say he actually tamed me. At last, I had found the man that I wanted my future children with.

Children, or a child, had always been on my 'to do' list. I wouldn't have said I was naturally maternal; in fact I often got called *cruella de ville*! However, once I had made my mind up, the burning desire deepened and consumed me. I was almost obsessed by the idea of having a baby and spent fortunes on pregnancy testing kits each month! Then, after a couple of devastating miscarriages, my dream came true! I was finally going to have a baby boy. My heart felt like it would burst, the love I had for my unborn child was already unconditional.

In reality, the build-up prior to, and during, my pregnancy was very stressful. My twin sister was seriously ill with depression.

Compiled By Kate Gardner

She was abusing alcohol, taking drugs, had attempted several overdoses, and was living on and off the streets. We were in the middle of moving house. Our current house was my partner's ex martial home. The last thing I wanted was to bring my newborn baby back there, as we had a lot of issues at the time with his ex, which added to the stress for us both. The new roof leaked, with water pouring down the walls in the middle of the night. The bathroom man left us mid job, work unfinished, with a toilet still on the landing, after being absconded to Spain on a murder charge! And on top of this, his mum threatened to take matters into her own hands when I dared to complain! I also wasn't sleeping a wink. Heavily pregnant, surrounded by stress in the hottest summer of 2006 was not a good combination! However, being a tough cookie. I still felt nothing would faze me; even the several panic attacks I had when our forthcoming house sale fell through did not slow me down.

I was totally not prepared for what was coming...

Bayley was born on the 21st August 2006 at Southend Hospital. It was a fairly uncomplicated 9lb 1oz birth, except for an episiotomy, which was something I really didn't want. I clearly remember them handing him to me, and rather than gushing feelings of love and joy that I had seen on television, I was completely engulfed with fear. Suddenly the massive responsibility of a newborn baby relying on me was hugely overwhelming.

3 weeks after feeding solidly 24/7 and not having time to brush my hair, clean my teeth or go to the toilet alone, I was showing signs of serious anxiety and mania, even asking my husband to use a secret code to prove he was real, so I could trust him.

My husband was getting extremely worried about my state of mind and called the health visitor. I was assessed by a doctor, and the next day ran out of the house barefoot screaming, before being taking to a psychiatric hospital and heavily medicated for postpartum psychosis. By this stage, I was completely delusional, hallucinating, paranoid and pretty much out of my mind.

3 nights and four long days I spent in hospital with other mentally ill patients, not postnatal mothers. It was a pretty scary place I can tell you that. A real living nightmare I can recall clearly. Everything was either in fast forward like on a horror film, or I was receiving subliminal messages through the TV, radio etc. I didn't trust a soul, as I believed they were trying to poison me, harm me, or rape me. My poor family was terrified. Devlin, my husband, brought the baby in daily, attempting to encourage me to continue breast feeding, although I had difficulty functioning at all.

One incident I remember is grabbing hold of the doctor. In my mind this was a nightmare, he was somehow my best friend's husband and if only I kissed him, I would wake up. Sadly not. Another time, I lay on the floor screaming like a toddler, again another attempt to shake myself awake! I even set off the fire alarm, screaming down the corridors there was a fire so we could all be let free. Fortunately, I can see the funny side now, however, at the time it was a different story. This nightmare was my living reality.

They finally let me home after convincing a panel I would not harm myself, or my baby. Justifying your sanity to a panel of strangers is no pleasant task, 'what do they want to hear' I kept asking myself, what on earth do I need to say to escape this hell? I then had up to 6 home visits a day to start, with continual questions and assessments. Sometimes, I would just walk away, unable to cope with it all. After 3 weeks I made a decision. However bad it would be, I was coming off the medication, it made me feel like a drugged up zombie, more confused than ever.

Compiled By Kate Gardner

I would learn to cope, learn to self-love and put my own oxygen mask on first, in order to be the amazing Mummy I had always dreamed of being. My son was my 'Why', my reason to recover.

A baby's many needs are great. However, if the Mummy literally cannot think straight, she is no good to anyone. As my mental state was so heightened, I quickly recognised the triggers that sent me over the edge. Lack of food sent my anxiety through the roof, I had to make sure I ate every 3 to 4 hours minimum. Exercise had a powerful effect too. I could literally speed walk off my anxiety, clear my mind and get the baby out of the house all at the same time! Another crucial element to self-love is sleep. Never underestimate the power of a nap, or a catch up if you haven't got a full night's sleep. It's crucial to your well-being and sanity.

Music became a useful tool in my armour; an effective way to lift my vibration and energy, power songs gave me strength, (I Will Survive, a favourite) Emotional songs helped me grieve following the death of my twin sister, 4 months after Bayley was born. (A whole other chapter to be written). My husband arranged a cleaner as the mess of the house would literally send me into a panic, and I had weekly visits to the beauty salon for various relaxation treatments. It took me a year of complete self-love and awareness of my thoughts and feelings, to get signed off the mental health register and I'm thankful for both their support and that of my husband, my rock.

Nearly 9 years later, life is pretty grand! Through discovering personal development and the law of attraction 3 years or so ago, I now teach others its power, and the importance of putting your own oxygen mask on first. Strangely enough, without knowing at the time, I had used the law of attraction and the power of the positive mind in my recovery. The first time I read the book The Secret, it really scared me knowing how real it was and how powerful our thoughts are! Nowadays, I'm not only happier emotionally and mentally, I'm also turning my passion into my purpose, earning a full time income while working part time from home, and teaching others to find their power within. My greatest joy is inspiring other to take action for change.

How else can we truly love others unconditionally, if we do not truly love ourselves first?

Compiled By Kate Gardner

Debbie McLaren

Debbie McLaren is a #1 International Best Selling Author with The Missing Piece Book Series, and a Speaker/Singer/Songwriter, awarded Semi-Finalist Placement in the 2015 Song of the Year Songwriting Contest. Deb's original songs will be on her new music website soon! Future plans also include a music/speaking ministry in churches and other venues.

Debbie's day job is working in the Human Services field helping others reach their goals and dreams. By the Grace of God, Debbie has 29 years of sobriety, and shares her experience, strength and hope with others that they too may find freedom!

You can reach Debbie at:

Email:
deb.mclaren@shaw.ca

Website:
http://debmclaren.com
http://debbiedmclaren.wix.com/author

Other:
soundcloud.com/debjmac
macjams.com/artist/debmac

The Missing Piece in Self-Love

Garfield and Nineteen Days
By Debbie McLaren

Staring at the Garfield bookmark that read, "I love me", I silenced the cry that was rising up from deep inside my soul. Smiled, accepted this gift of love, hugged and thanked the two little ones and entered treatment the following day. I was far from loving myself, in fact, just the opposite was true. I hated myself.

As my mind wandered back in time, I remembered liking myself as a youngster. Spending hours enjoying my own company, a vivid imagination taking me to dreams of what I would be when I grew up. You could find me on top of the haystack with a stick in hand for a microphone, belting out songs.

Sitting under a tree with scribbler and pencil in hand, a dream of writing my own books was born. Creating greeting cards, theme calendars, jewellery, dress designing, drawing, and painting kept me occupied a lot of the time. Some others weren't as excited about my projects and expressed harsh criticism. I internalized it and minimized my own talents and abilities to the point where I thought them meaningless and unimportant. I liked people and enjoyed their company too, always curious and genuinely interested in them, and would help if I could.

I didn't know if I had ever loved myself as Garfield's bookmark proclaimed. All the years of abuse, depression, drinking and drugs had lead me to a desolate place. I became a stranger to myself. A couple months before I entered an addiction treatment centre, I believe God gave me a vision of my future destination if

I continued on this way. I saw a glimpse of myself living in the gutter in the city. It was dark and black. I was so alone, lifeless and cold. Shook me to my core.

I prayed one night, "God, if you are real, I need you, please help me. Show me what to do." I went to sleep and woke up the following morning feeling a peace that surpasses all understanding.

A day later I discovered my car had a flat tire. I called a friend and he came over. His sparkling eyes, healthy complexion, confidence and contentment were obvious. He replied to my asking where he had been, "I went to a treatment centre and no longer drink or do drugs. I feel great." My answered prayer. I could barely speak as the tears were streaming down my face. I asked him if he would help me get to the treatment centre. He said "Yes." I realized into the 3rd day of being sober, God answered another prayer. The craving, compulsion and obsession for alcohol had vanished!! I no longer wanted or needed to drink, I was ecstatic!

In the treatment centre is where I began to love myself, Garfield would go with me everywhere I went. Counsellors encouraged us to value all the good about ourselves while also acknowledging and dealing with the not so good. The group sessions were beneficial as we heard positive feedback about ourselves from each other. The journey to self-love had begun. I made progress, but not enough.

Fast forward eight alcohol-free years…. I woke up in a hospital bed to the realization that my suicide attempt to end my life had failed. I was still alive, angry but alive. What had gone wrong? Simply put, I couldn't love myself while being caught in the cycle of abuse with seemingly no way out.

Nineteen days in the hospital was life changing for me. Doctors,

The Missing Piece in Self-Love

nurses, staff, clergy, some family, friends and relatives were God's hands and feet for the whole duration of my hospital stay. My younger brother arrived to stay with me when I was brought in by ambulance. That was a miracle he was available, he was about to leave on holidays. The main doctor, with tears in his eyes, said "Medically, you should not be here, it's a miracle you are alive. The amount of pills you took were in your system over 24 hours….we have no other explanation. He said that they were going to help me but, I needed to tell them right then why I tried to end my life. He said I was worth it. I was angry and replied, "You don't know me, (full of self-hate again) how can you say that?" To this he replied "Because I know you are worth saving". Warmth washed over my cold, hardened heart and years of tears came pouring out and I proceeded to tell him of the abuse in my life that had happened.

God's love and presence was so warm and loving, that my description of it will be inadequate. Think of the love you feel for those closest to you, the love you feel for someone so intensely, that kind of love that makes your heart beat, that human love… that love pales in comparison to God's love. With each gesture from someone on God's team, came this enveloping warm love that amazed me, left me in awe, speechless. Time after time, God's love flowed. The moment my Mom and Dad were telling my friend in the restaurant what happened, and the moment she was telling another friend in the gas station, enveloping warm love was gently loving my being. I confirmed these times with my friend, and they were exactly the precise time she was in conversation with them. God was waking me up to other's love for me, and sending His love along at every encounter. To summarize these events, I no sooner would have a thought of a need or request and it was answered with God's warm waves of love washing over me every time! The time Mom handed me our family Bible, I asked her how she knew I wanted it, it was just a thought in my head, she said, "I thought you might like this now." As the janitor came in the room the next day, she saw me reading the Bible and with a smile on her face said, "Keep reading that book, and you will be ok." Again, the warmth was present and she shared some of her story, "I know how it feels, and you will get through this." With each card, phone call, vase of flowers, letter from people, again, the same warmth was present. I couldn't help but start to love myself.

As God, the doctors and everyone were working so hard to keep me alive, I was told I wasn't out of the woods yet. I thought about talking to a pastor....moments later, in walks a pastor. We said the Lord's Prayer, he left the room and told my family I was going to make it. My memory is a little foggy at some of the time frame and order of events, but as my health deteriorated and I became disorientated, the doctors called my family in and said it was time for all to forgive one another and say what we needed to say, I might not make it through the night. I had taken a turn for the worst. We all forgave, prayed, hugged and cried. I needed rest. They left for the night and the next hour the nurses arrived to deliver some good news, "Your vitals are improving, your body is healing!!" Another miracle! These are only some of the miracles that took place that nineteen days.

As I drove home with Mom and Dad, I gazed at the beautiful blue sky and thanked God for all His love, forgiveness, and His hospital team. Also for helping myself, my family and friends deal with all this.

I knew I had to love myself, and that meant putting boundaries in place, accepting only healthy behaviours, actions and words from others, abuse was no longer a part of my life. Loving myself meant that even though I make mistakes, I don't mentally beat myself up

The Missing Piece in Self-Love

over them. Loving myself meant forgiving myself and others and keep moving forward. I acknowledge and change what needs to be changed. Keep my values and morals in check and live accordingly. I am not perfect, but I am loveable, I am not everything, but I am many things. I like myself today because I am true to myself which means that I follow God's lead with His love for me. Once I could accept all of me, I could love me. He made me with this personality, this creativity, this gift of music. I'm a people person and love to help others and also have fun! Today loving myself includes recording my original songs that will soon be on my new website, which is currently under construction. Also living the dream of being an author, now published in 5 books in the #1 International Best Selling Book Series - The Missing Piece! Today I still have the Garfield bookmark, and I can honestly say "I love me."

Compiled By Kate Gardner

Donna Porteous

Donna Porteous is a Metaphysician, an Intuitive and Health and LifeStyle Coach™. Her passion and background in health, science and spirituality has enabled her to integrate her innate gifts and practical wisdom into Soulful Living™.

As an Intuitive and Health and LifeStyle Coach, Donna applies nutrition and energy modalities, allowing our physical, mental, emotional and spiritually bodies to go beyond current beliefs and conditions to reach our dreams and goals with ease, ultimately enhancing our health, wealth, personal relationships and career lives.

Donna is from Ontario, Canada and facilitates consultations, events and retreats internationally.

You can reach Donna at:

Email:
donnadporteous@gmail.com

Facebook:
donna.porteous

The Missing Piece in Self-Love

The Game Changer
By Donna Porteous

There is a quote I love and live by from T. HarvEker, "How we do anything is how we do everything". This point of view aligns me with who I am, and what I am all about; love, freedom, ease, joy, glory, peace and clarity to live a life I desire verses settling. Dr. Wayne Dyer said, "When we change the way we look at things, the things we look at change" and the message from the movie *Patch Adams*, "Alter your perception, change your reality", makes us question how we are being with ourselves.

Harv's quote encourages me, yet can stop me in my tracks to pay attention to how I am being and what I am doing. I question myself, "Am I loving myself with gentleness, peacefulness or stressing with hurriedness and anxiety? Am I enjoying the process, being kind to me or is it just a means to an end for me?" Beware; our internal conversations are expressed as our physical life.

Once during a seminar exercise we were required to karate chop through a one inch board (I do not suggest doing this). The instructions were clear, it was a metaphor for life. If we normally stand back and observe life, perhaps we might want to volunteer to go first. This nailed me. I had to go first. I failed on my first attempt. I got all mentally psyched-up and centimeters before hitting the board, I pulled backed. I was terrified. I reassessed and repeated, "How I do anything is how I do everything". Where else was I doing this approach in life? I was determined to be successful at this challenge, because it was clear to me that it was a pivotal life principle. Well, let me tell you. My second approach was hysterical. Yes, I broke through that board. Not only did it split, but the sheer determination and power in my small body catapulted me about three feet up into the air, and about six feet across the room into the arms of a gentleman who caught me. I was shaking and trembling with joy beyond joy. Yes, I broke that board but most importantly, numerous old useless points of views and beliefs that were holding me back in my life were dissolved. So now I say with great conviction, "How I do anything, is how I do everything!" I learned to give it my all, to play life at a "10 plus" despite the fear, which is really False Evidence Appearing Real. This was my first big game changer into self-love.

This tool changed my reality. It expanded my awareness, elevated my frequency to vibrate with more joy, peace, appreciation and love for myself. I could feel the difference, the buzz inside of me. There is a scale of consciousness, one to a thousand, that measures this type of energy in megahertz by David Hawkins. The scale shows what feelings are equivalent to what vibration of energy. It shows that love is at 500 megahertz. This is important because the frequency of feeling and being love transforms, manifests and heals. How we do anything is how we do everything, right? Self-awareness is paramount, game changer number two.

This point of view is also a reference for doing small things with great love and the great things will look after themselves, as Mother Theresa taught. And in quantum physics, our outside world, the macro, is a reflection of our internal world of self-love, the micro. Knowing that our internal conversation produces results puts all the focus on self-love and awareness. It is reflected in everything that we attract. We demonstrate with our own way of how we be with ourselves, what we will accept, tolerate and allow from others. We literally teach others how to treat us. Authentic genuine self-love truly is the center of our universe. We can change the world one person at a time, starting with ourselves.

The Law of Attraction and Magnetism teaches that whatever and however we give our attention to, will be matched and returned with the same level and quality of intention. It does not decide what is right, wrong, good or not good for us. It merely matches our vibration, intention and frequency with the way we are feeling with life experiences. Note to self, this is game changer number three.

How you do anything is how you do everything. How do you love yourself? If you are not sure, take a look around you. Results are everywhere. Results are facts and do not lie. What is your environment like, how is your health and energy level, how are others treating you, how are they responding to your requests, do people like to sit beside you, are folks drawn to you to share positive loving stories or to complain? The answers to these questions are results and evidence of how you are loving yourself. They are not right, wrong, good or bad. They are results. How do these results make you feel? If the answers make you feel good inside, wonderful. If they do not, then perhaps a new game changer is in order.

One simple skill I use to change things up is to ask questions and do not come up with the answer. Let the answers show up instead. In 1996, I asked, more in desperation than anything as I sat down to sigh and muster up more courage to move ahead in life, "Please show me the secrets of the Universe and more importantly how to apply them to my life". Over the next several years, magic unfolded. I quickly learned to be all-inclusive and open with my questions and to ask the results to be with ease. Now I ask, "Show me how to integrate this wisdom in the highest and best way for me with ease, joy and glory, thank you". This is living in allowance. I love this fourth game changer.

As my courage and faith expands, life unfolds with wisdom and joy. I owe a huge thank you to all the people and experiences that have enriched my life. Many filled my missing pieces in self-love. The next transformational key was choosing an alkaline lifestyle and being trained as a pH nutritional microscopist with Dr. Robert Young. It not only gave me ultimate health and vibrancy but all the hundreds of people I work with have benefited beyond imagination. This was a huge stretch for me in every way possible and one with continuous returns.

Alkalinity, electron rich food; greens, healthy oils, proper amounts of alkaline water and coloured sea salt are all high frequency light and love, whereas as acidity, such as all sugars, starches and meat (hamburger is 3 MHz) emit low frequencies like fear and anger, irritating our cells. According to quantum physics, we are photons of light. We are alkaline by design, and emit acidity through function much like a car emits fumes when running. Also keep in mind that acidic thoughts, feelings, emotions and beliefs can add two-three times more acidity in our body than acidic food and liquids.

Like our world, we are over 70% water, and have over 6000 miles of vessels. Our intestinal track unfolded is 7200 square feet covering a tennis court floor. Our salty oceans need to have a pH of 8.3 to support life, just as our small intestinal track, our root system of health, needs to be 8.4 pH and our blood at 7.365 pH. We are salt water electrical acoustical magnetic beings; a salt water crystal system. All our fluids are salty; our tears, sweat, blood and endocrine system. We run on electrons not calories.

Upon raising my frequency with alkalinity; self-love, self-healing and life intensified. Living, loving and manifesting became way more fun and easier! I become healthier and more peaceful at a cellular and physical level. This is another perfect example of the micro, our cells and the macro, the whole person.

In life when we get the inside right, the outside shows the results. An alkaline lifestyle enhances all of our abilities to perform optimally; mentally, emotionally, physically and spiritually. It includes nutrition, keeping our internal channels of elimination clean and flowing (bowels, urination, sweating and breathe; did you know that our bowel has more brain cells than our brain; that our heart and brain waves are connected to the magnetic resonance of the earth and moon), exercise, perception, rest, play, connection to Spirit and Self. Living an alkaline lifestyle is the ultimate fifth game changer in self-love.

Our physical body reflects our mental approach to living and our emotional attitude towards life. I call it Soulful Living™. I invite you to contact me for assistance if you resonate with this wisdom. May you always nurture the living essence of splendour living within you, in all the ways that self-love calls you to enliven your soul.

Compiled By Kate Gardner

Ellis Panda

Hello! My name is Ellis, but my friends call me Panda. I'm 23, and live in the rainy UK!

I spend a lot of my time on social media, mainly posting and liking cute cat pictures, amongst other things, hehe!

I have a love for makeup, piercings, tattoos and anything that screams individuality and self-expression.

My goal in life is to be a change and spread good feelings through all the people I am fortunate enough to be connected with.

I hope that by sharing this life experience, it will encourage others to release their inhibitions and start on the journey of self-love!

You can find Ellis at:

Instagram:
@thisismyeden

Facebook:
www.facebook.com/EllisPandaOfficial

The Missing Piece in Self-Love

Loving Her to the Bones
By Ellis Panda

As I pushed the skin up around my eyes and tears rolled down my cheeks, I couldn't believe the mess I had become.

No matter how much I didn't eat, how much I didn't drink, I just seemed to get bigger and bigger. A troubled family life living with my grandparents forced the darkest of taints over my vision of the world, especially on how I viewed myself.

As the bullying I faced at school worsened, and any sort of support and interest from my family seemed non-existent, the only thing I could link it all to was my self-image. The pretty girls at my school never seemed to have any of this trouble. Why was I?

Every morning while getting ready for school, I stood and I put on my makeup, sighed heavily and went out to face the world. As what I ate got less and less, and my weight plummeted - which at the time I thought was great - I noticed the attention I got from people increased, but this time I thought it was in a good way. The likes and comments on my social media pages, Myspace and Bebo pages increased, and the attention I was receiving fuelled me to work harder to be what I thought was accepted.

At home, I was ridiculed for my size, my makeup, my hair, my dress sense. I couldn't win. The only thing I had complete control over was my weight. The battle between the aching hunger in my belly and keeping up this new found image was becoming hard. So I gave in, I ate. As I felt the food hit the bottom of my stomach, I was saturated in guilt. As good as it felt to ease the hunger, the fact I knew it'd make me gain weight was too much to bear. I took to sneaking off after meals and making myself sick. This way I got to eat and I got to stay attractive and thin, right?

This went on from some time and pretty soon my size 14 clothes were becoming too baggy, before I knew it I had plummeted to a size 6 and eventually a size 4 - beyond tiny for my 6 foot frame. It was great. I was getting attention from boys, made friends, but still every time I looked in the mirror, I was too big. I soon found myself in my first proper relationship in college and escaping from home for a few hours a day was such sweet release but still having someone to look good for was beginning to take its toll on me. I hated who I was. I seemed so fat, I was so lonely, and I was fast running out of ways to keep myself losing weight. I tried modelling to increase myself self-confidence. I couldn't understand why I'd only get the High Fashion shoots, then be stood in a room of gorgeous, slim models feeling like the sad, physical embodiment of the proverbial elephant in the room.

College dragged on and eventually I found myself finished. With nothing to show for it I took the first option they gave me, and went off to an art NVQ level course. It was in this time I met my current partner. We all dream of a knight in shining armour, and what I didn't know yet was that he was mine.

The tedious task of dragging myself backwards and forwards to my course became increasingly harder and harder. I struggled to get out of bed in the morning, my periods had stopped, I was exhausted. I was just turning 18 but I felt 80. I began having constant blackouts in the shower, even just from standing up. I felt like I was falling to pieces and I just couldn't figure out why. As things became more serious with my soon-to-be knight and I expanded my social horizons I once again found the pressure of outside eyes bearing down on me. I was spiralling out of control.

The Missing Piece in Self-Love

I dropped out of my course and spent my evenings smoking and drinking, to help me to numb myself long enough to forget about how I looked. It wasn't long until I found going back to my home life too much to handle. I had to get out. My grip on what was normal and what wasn't was slipping, and I didn't want to go out like this. One day I bagged up what little I had and left with the help of my partner and his family. No goodbyes, no sorrow, no let's talk this out, my grandparents shut the front door on me, and erased me from their lives.

I was alone.

Or so I thought.

The care and hospitality I received in my new home was like no other. I began eating and, with the support I received, I slowly gained a little weight, almost without noticing, climbing to a size 6/8. I remember getting ready and struggling to do up my jeans, they were tight - how did I let this happen? What if he sees I got fat and he doesn't want me anymore? Panic struck me and I felt physically sick.

Then he walks in, and I'm just stood there frozen like a deer in headlights, awaiting an insult. He grabs his shoes, looks me up and down and says 'you look good today baby', gives me a kiss and walks back out. I didn't understand, how? How can I look good, when I look like this?

I found myself in the house by myself a lot as I worked only a few days a week, one day boredom took over and I binged, sweets, biscuits, fizzy pop. It was amazing, I felt full. Actually physically full.

Then I felt guilty.

I dragged myself off to the bathroom to sort it the only way I knew how. As I knelt on the floor and faced the toilet bowl, I heard him. 'You look good today baby'. Then I heard every compliment he had ever given me, ones I realised I had taken no notice of before, and tears began falling from my eyes. I couldn't do it. I ran upstairs to our room to wipe my face and as I turned, I caught myself in the mirror.

There she was.

The tiny, fragile little girl I had become. Gaunt and pale. I lifted my top and saw my ribs, my hips. Look at her collarbones, the gap between her thighs, if you could even call them thighs. She was hunched over and she was terrified. She had been abused and neglected both physically and emotionally and she was banging on the mirror glass to be let out, to be helped. "I'm so exhausted, I can't do this anymore", she weeps.

As I pushed the skin up around my eyes and tears rolled down my cheeks, I couldn't believe the mess I had become.

I now look back and I can't believe I survived the way I did. I seem like someone else in my old photos. I don't know who I was, or what I was doing. I do know that the world will have no problem basing your self-worth on how you look and, when you do the same, it can be a very lonely way to live.

He saved my life, as did his family. Be careful what and how you say things to others, sometimes we do not realise how much of an impact the smallest comment or action can have on somebody's entire existence.

Self-love is hard. Self-love is getting up every morning, standing in front of the mirror and having the confidence to look yourself in the eye. Self-love is going out even when you don't feel great about your skin, or the way your hair looks. Its smiling in photos

The Missing Piece in Self-Love

even though you feel you're friends are better looking than you. It's spending time to get ready just so you can feel good about yourself.

You don't just wake up one day and love who you see. It's spending hours, days, even years, trying to become the person you want to be and why? Because you know deep down you deserve it.

That is truly loving yourself. Allowing yourself to simply be who or what you want to be and feeling how you want to feel.

Self-love is essential.

The world is full of people telling you that you're not good enough or pretty enough or even skinny enough.

Self-love is picking yourself up after all the negativity you experience

And allowing yourself to carry on.

I learnt the hard way, that you cannot expect others to love you unconditionally if you cannot love yourself in the same way. I was fortunate enough to find somebody who had enough love for the both of us, but sometimes all it takes is to look in the mirror and tell yourself that you are enough, you do matter and no matter what anybody says you are beautiful.

Compiled By Kate Gardner

Freyja P. Jensen

I'm an effervescent, polished Human Resources & Networking Professional, Relationship Manager, Recruitment Consultant, Public Speaker & Executive Ninja as well as a Mother, an Oma, a Daughter, Sister & valued friend. I believe our voices matter and that it's important to stand up and be heard. My mission is to advocate on behalf of those who have yet to find their voices, those struggling with Mental Health issues & about Suicide Prevention by bravely & openly sharing my personal experiences about overcoming the impossible, through Media and PR opportunities. I'm also a published writer and a 3 time International Best-selling Author.

You can reach Freyja at:

Email:
Freyja.Jensen@OpenForChange.com

LinkedIn:
www.linkedin.com/in/executiveninja

Twitter:
www.twitter.com/fpjays

Facebook:
www.facebook.com/norse.viking.goddess

Personal Email:
fpjays@live.ca

Compiled By Kate Gardner

Self-Love – My Awakening, My Salvation

By Freyja P. Jensen

This has, to this point, been one of the most difficult topics for me to write about. I'm great at encouraging, educating and empowering others on self-love but for me it has been a huge bone of contention. Perhaps feeling like I was not seen or heard as a child played a large factor in my evolution.

When I was a young girl about 9 years old my Father remarried following my Mother's tragic death, which I witnessed, and it traumatised me profoundly. My Mother to me was a most beautiful lady. In a young girl's eyes, she was the epitome of loveliness and I wanted to be just like her.

My Father was to have married my Step-Mother before he ever met my Mom. They grew up near each other in Germany and were to be married but she had declined at that time. He then went away to work elsewhere, met my Mother and fell madly in love. Following the tragedy of my Mother's death, ironically my step-mom bumped into my Father's parents in their home town and was told that their son was now a widower with 3 children. She had one son of her own and was divorced. They began corresponding, and Dad sent an invitation for them to come to Canada.

I recall times where she would be preparing her make-up and hair while I stood beside her in admiration, and she would comment that I had ugly lips and legs like my Mom. She would call my

The Missing Piece in Self-Love

Mother a whore and said that I would be just like her one day. Those words made me feel ugly and brought with it a deep sense of hurt that she was desecrating my Mother's image and wrecking mine. Wearing make-up for me was not an option until I left home. Though, there was a day in High School Home Economics Class when one of the "popular girls" offered to do my make-up. I was thrilled! I went home at lunch so proud and feeling beautiful, like the other girls. My Dad took one look at me and marched me to the bathroom, saying that if I wanted to look like a whore he would show me what that looked like. He took a tube of red lipstick and smeared it all over my face and said now you go to school. I was mortified. I wept pitifully all the way to a friend's nearby home to get help. They helped clean me up and I went to school feeling I would never fit in, because I was ugly.

Now I am aware that it was her own jealousy, and that the punishments I received came out of her anger. For my Dad, I believe he was very influenced by her anger. I remember one time when she dressed her own son like a girl to flaunt him in front of me, saying I wasn't her little girl because she already had one.

She didn't love me and my Dad didn't see me. I have come to realize that my parents were acting out their own pain, anger and losses through the punishments. They carried their pain and I paid the price. This has, in fact, affected me my entire life. Feeling like I was not pretty or smart or would amount to anything was ingrained into my head, heart and my soul and identified later in life as mental illness.

Years of self-help, personal development, countless hours with counselors and therapists confirmed that it was not me that was broken, and that I could in fact take back and own my own power and self-esteem. I have learned that I am an amazing person and beautiful in my own way, just the way I am. We all need to accept and believe that we are perfectly imperfect.

Within the year that I was 49-50, I was discovered by a Photographer who felt that I would be a beautiful muse and desired to have me in front of his camera. I became absorbed in seeing myself flourish and bloom and discovered a new me. Someone whose smile brought joy to others, whose body image drew attention and admiration from many suitors and fans, whose legs were chosen for stocking advertisements and I became somewhat of a celebrity pin-up model at 50! That certainly changed things from what my self-image once was.

When I put on weight during my menopausal period this past year, a self-loathing arose within me again, I won't be liked, loved or wanted because I don't fit the mold. I started declining, withdrawing, and feeling unworthy. Again! Everyone is visual, men in particular and when I heard that "it can't be helped" that is who we are, and don't blame me, it's part of our biological make-up, I fought back. Look in the mirror, men and ladies. No one is perfect, and I most certainly realize I am not and with that, the A-HA moment; that being imperfect is perfectly okay.

I feel like I have awakened during the writing of this chapter with the realization that Self-Love is acceptance of being okay just as we are and that we need no one's approval but our own. It took writing about it to bring it all to life.

I have Post Traumatic Stress Disorder and with it, anxiety, panic, depression and more. Some days are very good and some horribly bad. In spite of it all I have an acute awareness that I am here for a reason and that the world needs me. I am embarking on a major shift in my journey, following my heart.

The Missing Piece in Self-Love

As part of the Mental Health board in Ottawa I am taking on speaking engagements for youth and adults, to bring awareness to Mental Health issues and to provide options to those struggling with mental illness or suicide. No one needs to go through dark times alone, there is help available. With that, I am also championing the Semi-Colon project locally; an endeavor to bring awareness to suicide prevention.

I have been in many relationships, 3 marriages and 8 engagements. I am a lover not a fighter so when issues would arise and I felt unloved, disrespected and dishonored, I would go through the FFF cycle, fright, fight & then flight. In several instances, I was at the point of committing suicide. I had many plans of exactly where I would drive off of the road. From the time I was a child being humiliated, degraded and abused I felt that there was something wrong with me. I felt it was my fault and it led me down some vicious paths, where I made some seriously bad choices, ones that I am ashamed of and also those that were just plain dumb. All I wanted was love, to be loved, seen, heard and valued, just the way I am. My son being on this earth kept me alive and it was my responsibility to him to do the best I could. Because his Father had moved to another province when my son was 4, finding a partner for me was one thing but I also wanted him to have a solid male presence in his life to look up to that would be there for him. I wanted the best for him, and for him to know that he was not alone. I did the best with what I had, knew and was capable of. Very recently I got myself a 'semi-colon' tattoo with my son and grand-daughters name beside it to pay homage to my courage in staying alive.

A semi-colon is used when an author could've chosen to end their sentence, but chose not to. The Author is YOU and the sentence is your life. The stigma around mental illness is very real, and has many barriers for those needing help. I've faced dark times, but

Compiled By Kate Gardner

I'm still here. It is my mission to advocate and spread awareness on these subjects.

Here is what I want to say to you; we all want to be loved as we are, for who we are from the inside out. Forget the wrapping I always say, as it is just pretty packaging. What's of value is on the inside, our heart and soul. A true relationship is about accepting each other without judgement, unconditionally. That's all I've ever wanted and that is what I want for you. We don't have to look outside of ourselves for strength, courage or love, as everything we need is found within. We just need to dig deep to get there sometimes.

I am finally at a place in my life where I know that, in order to feel worthy, I merely need to look inside of myself. I am love, loveable and worth loving and so are you. Self-love is the key and the ticket to being our healthiest selves and we can't be of value to anyone else without valuing ourselves first. My journey has brought me to this realization and it is my salvation.

JAMBO; I am glad our paths have crossed on this great adventure called life.

Wishing you much peace, joy and rainbow heart self-love.

Freyja P. Jensen

The Missing Piece in Self-Love

Greg Fletcher

Greg is a father, friend, tai chi instructor, musician, photographer, healer, writer, meditator, sonic engineer, etc.

But really, he's simply another person currently residing on planet Earth just like you.

He's spent many years fine tuning his main purpose of existence, which is to try and improve our ability to love simply being alive.

The methods that Greg uses are generally based on Taoist (pronounced with a D as in Dow) teachings, as he has always found them very practical and super applicable to real world living.

Also, he loves you unconditionally!

You can reach Greg at:

Website:
http://sp00fraydius.weebly.com/

Email:
taichilife@gmx.com

Compiled By Kate Gardner

You Are a Miracle

By Greg Fletcher

You are a miracle.

The very simple fact that you're here now, reading these words, backs me up. You are a miracle.

Speaking from my humble Taoist perspective, I believe that self-love, or being in love with yourself first and foremost, is actually the default natural state. I'm not talking about an egotistical, conceited, self-absorbed state. I'm talking about the energy (chi) that generates, animates and stimulates everything, everywhere, being of pure love.

But, due to a whole slew of different possible reasons, we can often find ourselves a little lacking in this most beautiful awareness.

You are a miracle.

How are you even here?

If you think back to all the myriad events that have happened in your life since you first entered this world, I reckon you'd probably find yourself in a state of amazement at just how much you've been through over the years, the hardships that you've endured and conversely, the achievements that you've accomplished... All to get to this very moment, right now.

There have probably been times when you found yourself completely and utterly unsure how you were ever going to carry

The Missing Piece in Self-Love

on, to get through... Yet, you did. You have. And here you are to prove it.

You are a miracle (repeat 3 times 'I am a miracle').

I reckon that it's worth spending a few moments just letting those words sink in deep.

In fact, for a few moments, let's try to help those words on their journey by trying to drop any psycho-physical/emotional armor that may, or may not, be there. Let's relax...

If I asked you to relax, what would that mean to you?

I'm sure that you'd have a shed load of answers for me, but I wonder if most of them are actually not relaxing in the true sense. They might be just different activities to what you'd be doing if you weren't 'relaxing'. To really relax, actually means to release tension (normally muscular tension) and to soften, to sink.

So with that in mind, (please just bear with me here) maybe have a go at this:

If you can, sit comfortably on a chair with your feet flat on the ground. Using your belly to expand and contract as you breathe in and out, allow your breathing to become smooth, even, fluid and relaxed. There is a saying that 'the quality of your breathing affects the quality of your thoughts' and vice versa. Drop your shoulders, raise the crown of your head just slightly. Slowly scan your body from head to toes for any muscular tension that might be there, and if found, it's absolutely fine to allow it to dissipate and release. In other words, relax...

Now, this time, allow these 4 simple words to really resonate (I love that word) within you: 'I am a miracle' (repeat a few more times 'I am a miracle'). Place extra emphasis on a different one of the 4 words each time you repeat the phrase. You don't have to say the words out loud if it's perhaps inappropriate to currently do so... It's the intent that matters.

You may also, if you wish, increase the potency of the effect by writing the same 4 words down 9 times.

How do you feel now?

What we're obviously trying to get to happen here, is to get those wonderful 4 words to find their way into your mental mainframe, as it were, using various methods of repetition. All whilst in a mindful, open, receptive, and relaxed state of being.

I believe there can be a potential risk that simply reading more and more very clever philosophical writings from some very wise dudes may well end up as an enjoyable intellectual pursuit but, possibly, without much overall benefit to one's day to day existence.

Therefore, if you find yourself brushing up on some deep and meaningful literature, engaging in some kind of mindful exercise, i.e. something that requires you to pay attention to your entire being, will, if done alongside the philosophy, probably help a whole bunch.

Obviously, as a long time practitioner and teacher of the form, I would highly recommend the Taoist art of Tai Chi Chuan as it's been designed to actually balance the whole body and mind, encouraging more energy (chi) to be cultivated and circulated throughout the entire somatic architecture. It's great stuff..!

Although, one does have to pick carefully, as Tai Chi seems to have become somewhat watered down nowadays, probably in an attempt by some well-meaning folks to make it super easy for people to play. Which can end up removing the reasons that it normally works so well, both as a healing art and a self-defense form. I believe, for it to work its magic, Tai Chi should be difficult!

The reason the Taoists hold so much stock in balancing yourself physically and energetically (chi), is that emotional and psychological harmony tends to happen as a result. The five vital organs; the heart, liver, spleen, lungs and the kidneys are all responsible for various emotional states. So by using Tai Chi or Chi gong etc, the harmony and balance can be found and maintained. But alas, I digress…

Let's get back to it:

You are a miracle (repeat 'I am a miracle').

I'm sure like me, you've had your fair share of reflective moments, and whilst you were having one of those, maybe you noticed that there are lots of people that you love in this life. People such as your family, friends, your colleagues, and your peers etc. Perhaps people who've inspired you or do inspire you from all over the world.

But, perhaps the most important and often, hardest person to unconditionally bestow your love upon, is your very good self.

There are a multitude of possible reasons for this but it is, nonetheless, a humongous error because:

You are a miracle (repeat 'I am a miracle').

You, are the first person that should warrant your unconditional love. You, are the person that has always been there, through every single experience…

You are a miracle (repeat 'I am a miracle').

I'm sure that it's only my daily discipline of tai chi and mindfulness that has slowly taught me to become more or less relaxed and happy and, yeah, with moments of untarnished joy thrown in!

For instance, years and years ago when I first started to learn the tai chi and Taoist teachings, I would catch myself suddenly noticing a moment or two here and there when I actually felt relaxed and not stressed. But nowadays it's the reverse and I'm very, very grateful for it.

I still get pissed off and have fabulous moments of childish outbursts here and there, but I've learnt to enjoy them for what they are, they remind me that I'm alive. They're only feelings anyway... Just energy. It can always be used for something else instead...

Feeling anything, whatever it might be, is fine as long as one enjoys that feeling. Once it's not enjoyable, one is always allowed to stop feeling it and choose to experience something else. You are not obliged to spend any time, at all, feeling an emotion if you're not actually enjoying it. You are not the emotion...

Loving yourself is surely only ever going to have a positive effect on whatever you're doing in life, including what you get out of life and, by extension, what you give back to life?

There is no reason whatsoever that you shouldn't love yourself.

You are a miracle (repeat 'I am a miracle') and how could anyone not love a miracle?

Whatever has happened in the past, which is a very shady area anyway, is just that. It might be helpful to consider that there is no past and also no future. Only this very moment right now. Everything, revolves around this very moment.

The Missing Piece in Self-Love

Being in love with yourself (an underlying state of love), first and foremost is, at your core, how you naturally want to be. It's peace. A state of grace if you will. It's home.

This doesn't imply being superficially perfect at all, it means being human and in full acceptance of that and all that goes along with that.

It actually requires you to use up lots of energy by not loving yourself. Crazy huh? Either by the physical tension that you may be holding somewhere, or the psychological and emotional tension.

We all have times when we do it. I'm no stranger to those various negative feelings that can show up here and there, but I have now learnt to be aware of them and how they feel if they show up (which they do occasionally). The trick for me, is to not fight them as this only adds more stress and tension, thus giving them more power and control.

So, if you find yourself being hassled by feelings of stress, tension and/or unenjoyable emotions, then maybe thank them for being yet another reminder that you're alive. And then, after checking your breathing, remind yourself of just how truly great you really are.

After all,

You are a miracle (repeat 'I am a miracle').

Compiled By Kate Gardner

Jennifer Insignares

Jennifer Insignares is the founder and CEO of Designs by Jen. She's also the official Graphic Designer of the #1 International Best Selling Book Series, The Missing Piece.

She works with clients to develop their vision and creates high quality custom designs that truly impress. With a unique gift of really getting into the client's mind to create designs exactly as the client saw them, or even better than they could imagine.

Jennifer's ultimate goal is to turn your vision into reality with design. Creating designs that will attract the right clients to your business.

You can contact Jennifer at:

Website:
www.yourdesignsbyjen.com

Email:
yourdesignsbyjen@gmail.com

Facebook:
www.facebook.com/creativedesignsbyjen

The Missing Piece in Self-Love

From Rock Bottom to Self-love
By Jennifer Insignares

Today you may look at me and see a powerful, confident, successful woman, but my story definitely didn't start out like that. For as long as I can remember, up until a couple of years ago, I was a very anxious and fearful person. Afraid to try anything new because of the possibility of messing up, failing or just saying something stupid and having someone laugh at me. It was so bad I wouldn't even pick up the phone when someone called because, what if I didn't understand what they wanted and didn't know how to answer their questions? I didn't want to embarrass myself.

So fast forward 30 years, this scared, anxious, shy girl, now a woman, I found myself hitting rock bottom. I had just moved from Brooklyn, New York to Los Angeles, California. The guy I had been with for 8 years, and married to for two of those years, just left me in LA on our two year wedding anniversary to head to Oakland, California for work. Two months prior to this, I found out he had been cheating on me with multiple women while I was helping to support him through school. We went through some counselling before we moved, and I made the decision that I wasn't going to give up on our marriage. I was willing to fight to try to stay together. I chose to move to LA so I would at least see him every month when he came down to work in LA from Oakland. I couldn't bring myself to move to Oakland where he had cheated on me. We agreed that we would start dating each other again, to bring us back together.

Here I am in a brand new city with no friends, no family, no husband, no job and no place to live. The place I was supposed to move into I thought was going to be ready when I got there, but it turned out she didn't need me to move in for 30 days. Desperate and trying to think of what I was going to do, I remembered my cousin had a friend who lived in LA that said I could crash on her couch for a week if I needed to. I reached out to her and asked if the offer was still available and if we could extend my stay for a month. Without hesitation she said yes. As soon as she got home from work that day I went on over, unpacked the few things I had in my car, and started my crazy journey to self-love.

The entire month I was there I searched for work in the graphic design and printing fields. I came across a direct marketing company that helped people with health, fitness, mindset and sales. They were willing to train me, and I got invited down to see what it was all about. When I walked in the room, I could feel the energy and see the excitement on everyone's faces. I didn't know much about the company, but I knew in that moment I wanted to be a part of it. I signed up that day and started going to every event possible. After about a month or so I realized the company was very much focused on personal development. Something I was so hungry for with all the changes that were going on in my life at that point. I started doing 15 minutes to an hour of personal development a day. Any classes, seminars or events I could go to, I was there. Motivation Mondays, Women Empowerment Wednesdays, seminars on the weekends, surrounding myself with so many incredible, positive people.

The events were incredible. Then, I would go home by myself every night. I was extremely lonely and some nights I would cry myself to sleep, thinking about the crazy changes that were happening in my life. I was still trying to work on my marriage, and moved four different times in the span of a year. There were days that I wanted to give up. Days when I didn't even want to get out of bed. Somewhere inside myself I found the strength to continue to get up and focus on me.

I had decided I was tired of being afraid and anxious all of the time. This was the first time in my life that I was being pushed so far out of my comfort zone. One of my biggest fears was public speaking. I made a commitment to myself that no matter what, I would get up and say something at every event, especially if it made me feel uncomfortable. And I did.

After a special 5-day intensive where I faced many of the things that I feared and where many blocks were removed, something shifted inside me. I began to feel more confident and comfortable in my own skin. On a mission to help myself and inspire others, I started sharing my journey on social media. **I lost 30 lbs. and I was back in clothes I hadn't worn since high school.** It had been about a year and I was finding myself again. I was looking good, and feeling good about myself, in spite of what was going on between me and my husband.

I found my passion for dance again, and I joined one of the groups in the company that was teaching a Salsa Fit Class. I was there every week, eventually getting up on stage to help teach the class. I also got certified as a Zumba instructor and I took on public speaking, something that had always terrified me.

Then, one day at one of my women empowerment events, I met an incredible mentor and friend. She could see past my smile and saw right through to the hurt I was feeling inside, and that I tried so hard to hide. We stayed over an hour after the event chatting about what was going on in my personal life with my husband. One thing that came up during it conversation was that I was a graphic designer. We exchanged information and, later that evening, she contacted me with a proposition.

She is a psychologist and said that if I would do some graphic work for her, then she would do a weekly call with me to help me with all the hurt, betrayal and abandonment I was feeling. I thought this was perfect! Now all the work I had been doing on my own I could do with a professional, and we could go even deeper than I could ever go on my own. I accepted, and every Thursday we had a call. Whenever she needed anything designed I took care of it. This was the start of my very own business, Designs by Jen, something that I had wanted for a very long time.

Unfortunately, my husband eventually decided he no longer wanted to be with me. It was very difficult to accept his decision after I had tried so hard to make it work. We are currently in the process of getting a divorce. As difficult as it has been, I wouldn't change a thing because it brought me to where I am today. I found myself again.

Using everything that I have learned on my journey, putting myself out there, getting uncomfortable, meeting new people, going to new events and networking myself and my business, I began to build my amazing company which led me right here, to The Missing Piece company with Kate Gardner. I am now her official graphic designer and still working on pushing myself out of my comfort zone to share my journey with you.

I can't say that my journey is finished. I think for me it is a continuous thing. Some days I may not feel my greatest. Some days I can be hard on myself. But I get to wake up every day, and choose to love myself. Love the process, love the journey. You really never know what might be around the corner.

The Missing Piece in Self-Love

Kirsty Holland

Originally from the UK, Kirsty currently lives in San Diego. Throughout an award-winning career spanning both retail and property management, and now online business, Kirsty quickly made the connection that how she felt about herself was paramount in how effective she was at connecting and communicating with others.

Through turbulent times, including the loss of her firstborn son to SIDS, divorce, and living overseas, the connection remained the same. How effectively you deal with any kind of life experience comes down to how you feel about yourself!

Kirsty is an International Best Selling Author, Speaker, Video Blog Host, and a Sales Integrity Strategist. She loves teaching entrepreneurs how to sell effortlessly online (without the 'icky' factor) incorporating all of the behind the scenes 'stuff' that makes everything you learn in business school fall into place! She also provides Concierge Social Media Solutions for business owners with busy schedules.

Compiled By Kate Gardner

You can reach Kirsty at:

Website:
www.kirstyholland.com

Email:
Grace@graceinthesun.com

Facebook:
www.facebook.com/GraceintheSun

The Missing Piece in Self-Love

A Woman, Rising

By Kirsty Holland

She felt the tears begin to prick her eyes. Determined not to let them fall, she turned her back and pretended to laugh along, then went back to hiding inside of herself. "If you didn't have hands, would you wear gloves?"...."no", she answered. "Well, why do you wear a bra then?" He continued, as he laughed at his own joke. It was a familiar one to her, and when she'd mentioned that it hurt her feelings, her husband had simply said he was 'only joking ' and 'didn't really mean it'. She felt unloved, and unheard, her feelings, quite obviously, were not being taken into account.

This, and other 'jokes' made at her expense were not new to her, she'd come from a background of cruel comments and negative remarks.

"They aren't looking for plain girls like you, you're not pretty enough. Don't waste your time' she was told, when asking her mother if she could enter a competition to model during her teenage years. This compounded the comments from earlier in her childhood, like the time she wanted to audition for a local production of 'Annie', her favorite musical. "You won't get a part, so why bother". These, and many more comments that, ultimately, damaged her self-confidence, self-esteem, self-worth, self-love...anything that defined her as who she was, served to strip away any ounce of respect or ambition she had for herself. The cherry on the top was 'you'll never amount to anything'. These words echoed in her heart throughout the years to come.

When she suffered a miscarriage in March of 1991, just three months after the death of her firstborn son to Sudden Infant Death Syndrome (Cot Death), her mother-in-law said to her "of course you miscarried on my birthday! And it's Mother's Day! Can't you do anything right?!" On top of the guilt and devastation she already felt, now she was being blamed for not giving her husband a baby. Alongside this, her husband himself blamed her for their son's death. Despite moving forward and giving it her best, that marriage would eventually come to an end, but not before physical and emotional abuse became her norm.

As her marriage fell apart, she found herself a single mum with children under five. She moved back to the village her parents lived in, after they offered her help and support during the separation. It didn't take long before her mother started reminding her of all that she wasn't. "Who do you think will want you now, you're damaged goods. Divorced and with children" and "you're not exactly a catch now, are you?"

Her life seemed to pick up after she met her second husband a couple of years later. An American in the U.S. Navy, he was stationed in the UK for three years. Her parents seemed surprised when she said she had met someone. They were even more surprised when she bought him home to meet them, and discovered he was Black. Her father, an extremely racist and bigoted man, got up and walked out of the room. Her Grandmother muttered "Your Grandpa will be turning in his grave", and her mother, very surprisingly, seemed calm about the whole series of events.

She would later show her true colors, however. They never stayed hidden very long. She knew that well, and prepared herself for the onslaught of nastiness that she knew would inevitably follow. Especially when she discovered she was pregnant. "Think about

The Missing Piece in Self-Love

the children, the Blacks don't accept them, and the Whites don't want them" her mother declared. Quickly followed by "You better hope this marriage works out, because there won't be any decent man that will want you after this" - 'this' referring to her interracial relationship, and the two bi-racial children that were born during that time.

Sadly, that marriage was doomed to fail too. Months into dating, she knew he was still meeting people online. Throughout their seven years together, that was a behavior that would continue, and when coupled with the lies and deceit, was more than she could bear to take. Especially given that the relationship had come with immense personal sacrifice (a whole other book!)

Finding herself alone and a single parent again, living in the U.S, almost 6,000 miles from anything or anyone familiar, she knew things had to change. Something inside told her that the change started there. It had to start with her.

As she looked back through the various closed chapters in her life, and tried to make sense of why all of this had happened, a thought occurred to her. "I don't like this place. I'm not a victim. Surely all of these things can't possibly be my fault?" Slowly, as she allowed and acknowledged each experience to surface, and felt the emotions that came with it, as fresh as the day she first felt them, she began to unravel each story she had been told. Each negative belief that had been forced upon her, and that she had ended up taking on as her own.

She felt her heart close to the possibility of ever being in love, telling herself 'it just wasn't out there for her', another mind-made story that would prove to be untrue, although some time down the line. She threw herself into raising her children and working to support them. Every day she became more involved with personal growth and, not afraid to show up and do the necessary work on herself, she began to look at things differently and chose to see herself in a more positive way. To see her shadows and dance with them joyfully, accepting them as simply a part of herself to also be loved and forgiven.

It's been almost eight years since the end of her second marriage, and her realization that everything couldn't possibly be her fault! If you were to ask anyone who knows her, they would tell you that she is one of the most genuinely beautiful people, not just physically but down to her soul, and that her upbringing and life experiences must have been some of the best! But they would have fallen into the belief that a person's past defines their future. Little do any of them know that, like a great Phoenix, sometimes self-destruction is the only way you can learn to rise from the ashes.

One aspect of the personal sacrifice mentioned earlier in this chapter, was the estrangement from her then 10 year old daughter. Her daughter had remained in England under the guidance of her grandparents, after her second husband's military posting took them to Japan. Her mother, once again, had her own agenda for allowing this, and sought to destroy the relationship between her and her daughter during the posting overseas. This was a relationship that was not allowed to find footing again until her daughter was sixteen, and they connected on social media. And, as before, this was only possible by learning to burn the bridges and walk away, releasing any humility bestowed upon the situation, and forgiving herself.

The self-love she found continues to spill over into every aspect of her life. After only seeing her eldest daughter on video messenger for the last seven years, the Phoenix within her quite literally rose and took flight, and a trip home to the UK in May of

2015 - her first trip back in almost thirteen years - culminated in them finally reuniting in person.

It was only through learning to love herself enough that she has been able to give herself the things she deserves, which includes rebuilding a now-unshakeable relationship with her daughter. During this rebuilding process, and the inevitable sharing that comes with it, she learned of her daughter's struggles during the time with her grandparents, so similar in nature to what she, herself, had endured. You can learn a little about her daughter, Ellis, and some of her experience by reading her chapter in this book -'Loving Her To The Bones'.

Writing this chapter has been an act of deep self-love. Continuing to acknowledge that, although we can easily get pulled back into the stories of our past, they are just that - stories. When it seems easier to fall back into our familiar forlorn state of mind, it's then we need to love ourselves enough to stand up and fiercely own our truth, imperfections and all. Our past in no way defines us, and we have opportunities and the right to choose self-love daily.

Compiled By Kate Gardner

Laurie Reid, LMFT, CAP

Laurie Reid is CEO and Founder of **Breaking the Cycle Consulting,** she's a Child to Parent Violence expert, who provides **insightful and innovative solutions and training** for families who are experiencing teen aggression.

An award winning therapist, Laurie's extensive experience was based in her 18 year background-- as a Southwest Asia Bronze Star Medal Recipient while in the **US Navy** and as a therapist, addiction professional and coach.

She's an author, and speaker who's had numerous interviews for national **television, radio** and **print (She was featured in the Orlando Sentinel, and on Fox!)** and has presented at numerous therapy conferences.

You can reach at Laurie at:

Website:
www.ChildtoParentViolence.com
www.BreakingtheCycleConsulting.com

Facebook:
www.facebook.com/BTCconsulting

The Missing Piece in Self-Love

LinkedIn:
www.linkedin.com/in/lauriereid

Email:
breakingthecycle@contractor.net

Compiled By Kate Gardner

My Journey to Self-Love
By Laurie Reid

I remember when I was a young girl, my father, a Vietnam veteran, would barricade himself in the basement nightly, armed with a six pack and the TV remote. It could have been because he just wanted to be alone to drink, or maybe because he wanted to avoid all the drama happening upstairs between his bi-polar wife and moody adolescent daughters. Probably both. I remember I was told not to disturb him because he worked hard all day and needed, no *deserved*, this time alone.

Despite this self-imposed isolation, I managed to have a close relationship with my dad. I worked hard to become his favorite—the one who went with him to do "guy" things, like hunting and fishing, eschewing typical female pastimes like fussing with hair and make-up. Nothing made me happier than when he included me. Not only was he a real life hero, he was my hero. I worked hard to win over his love and attention.

It was no real surprise, then, when at age 17, I followed in my dad's and my grandfathers' footsteps and joined the military. As part of a penance for getting caught shoplifting with my best friend (who is still my best friend), I was serving community service time working at the local Navy recruiting office. It wasn't difficult for them to recruit me, as I was pretty much the Uncle Sam's "We Want You" poster child. I wanted so badly to be wanted, though I didn't realize it at the time, much less know how to express such powerful feelings.

The Missing Piece in Self-Love

As with my dad, I knew the best way to feel accepted was to conform to others expectations of me. In the military, conforming is a given. Unfortunately, neither of these experiences taught me a damn thing about self-love. In fact, love of self was discouraged, both at home and in the service. It wasn't even on my radar screen.

I remember being on an aircraft carrier in the middle of the Persian Gulf—one of the first women in that position—and feeling sick to my stomach, aching in my back, and having severe anxiety. I knew I could not succumb to these feelings. My personal needs, even pressing physical ones, were subordinate to the needs of others and duty. My job required me to "suck it up, sailor." Taking action to care for myself would have been viewed not only as selfish, but worse, as "weak."

Perhaps the first really 'selfish' thing I did was to marry my husband, another military man, and then to make the decision to remain child free. Together, we decided and preferred to focus only on each other and on our careers. We spent many, many nights working late, even checking emails while on vacation, and doing whatever it took to be successful.

It worked, too. We made an insane amount of money, maxed out our retirement accounts, saved for pre-retirement years and bought three homes all before the age of forty. On top of my corporate job, I also opened my own consulting company, Breaking the Cycle Consulting, a company devoted to breaking the cycle of teen aggression and violence. Ambitious and driven were words that described me whenever I completed a personality quiz on Facebook.

From the outside looking in, it seemed we had everything. Every night there we would be, sitting in the same room, each completely absorbed in our laptops or staring at the television, cocktails on coasters next to each of us.

But something was wrong. At first, I could not put my finger on it. One night, though, I looked over at my husband—the love of my life—and I saw how much weight he had gained, how heavily he was drinking, how absorbed he was 'zoning out' in front of the TV or on his work phone, and it struck me how much he reminded me of my father. This man with whom I once felt so connected, now was remote, shut down and emotionally unavailable.

And then I turned my gaze inward. Years earlier, to try and understand my crazy childhood, I had become a therapist and an addictions counselor. I was so self-assured, smug almost. I felt comfortable in chaos. Yet, here, suddenly, on a hot South Florida night in my own living room, my childhood rose up and one, two punched me in the gut:

"I had married my father."

"Was I now destined to become my mother?"

As terrified as I was to have the hard conversation with my husband, to share with him my deep dissatisfaction, I was even more terrified of what would happen if I did not. So I asked him to put down his phone, put away the remote and set aside the drink. I did the same. Instead, we sat on the patio overlooking the pool, side-by-side, not yet ready to face one another, and I took a deep breath and said: "We can't do this anymore. Our well-being matters. You matter. *I matter.*"

That moment of courage, of taking a stand for myself and my needs, was the start of many conversations. Conversations that, ultimately, led us to the decision to completely upend our lives. Soon, we fled the bustle and bright lights of South Florida for a small farm community in rural North Georgia, setting up house in the cabin we bought for retirement.

The Missing Piece in Self-Love

At first, it was not my glass of Southern sweet tea, to say the least. I feared losing all I had achieved, especially the prestige of my corporate job. All my life I had lived only for approval and acknowledgement. My friends and colleagues chided me, telling me how bad this decision would be for my career, how bored I would be living in the country, without fine dining, cultural activities and access to shopping (the nearest store is over an hour away). I worried mostly about winter, though. Would I be holed up, snowbound with only the darkness of my thoughts? Would the depression I had kept at bay for so many years with sunshine, busyness and work once again descend over me?

Thankfully, it has not. Although day-to-day life seems to have slowed a bit, my days feel fuller somehow. Both my husband and I work from home. We spend lots of time together enjoying the beauty of the Blue Ridge Mountains. We've found a church community we love. I'm also now better able to focus on my consulting company, and helping more families overcome the cycle of teen aggression, which is my life's mission. I live each day with purpose, not panic.

These days, instead of drinking like fish, we knock off work early and go fishing. We no longer sit in the same room, ignoring each other and our emotional pain, and pretending we love our lives.

From the moment I was able to acknowledge to myself, and then to my husband, that my feelings matter, my needs were not being met, and I needed and deserved more, the trajectory of my life changed forever. No longer do I live in fear, or for accolades and approval. Now, I live only for love, of God, my husband, my new home, and, at long last, myself.

Compiled By Kate Gardner

Leigh Burton

Although life is a never ending source of chapters in our journey, this chapter in mine was pinnacle. I know that I will never be able to go back to the person I was before and, as a result, decided to make a life for myself that would reflect that. Although I had a great career as a nurse, and was already a third of the way through a Bachelor's degree in nursing, I made the decision to walk away. I gave it all up, and decided to fill my life with the things that I am most passionate about. Travel and helping others. Now I go to work every day doing something that isn't work at all. I continue to write, and I manage my own retreat business. I frequently travel to the Mayan Riviera - my personal favourite part of Mexico, where I share the wisdom of the ancient Toltec. Helping people love themselves enough to love themselves better. A week of being treated the way that they should treat themselves. From the moment they land in Cancun, they are treated as the VIP that they all are. Enjoying the beauty of the Mayan Riviera, visiting ancient archaeology, learning about the culture of the Maya, and gently finding the key to unconditional self-love. Oh, and a visit with a local shaman doesn't hurt. Feel free to visit my website for further writing that I share, and see for yourself how to love your life, and live well...

The Missing Piece in Self-Love

You can reach Leigh at:

Website:
www.soulintentions.ca

Compiled By Kate Gardner

You're Perfectly Human
By Leigh Burton

After a journey to Teotihuacan Mexico, my life was changed forever. It was a trip I decided to take because I somehow knew that it was going to give me my missing piece in self-love. It was a place where I made a pact with the Universe. "For the truth, I will share the truth." These are the exact words that I said as an offering at the portal, in the Temple of the Jaguar. The "truth" by the way, is what I call the way of life practiced by an ancient society called Toltec. The word Toltec means artist, and they believed that with a particular way of thinking, you can create your life as heaven on earth, and they are right. I have since then loved the life that I am in, instead of continuously searching for a magic key to a life that I could never find.

As is yours, my life has been filled with chapters to what is my journey. Some of which are good, but most not so good. I spent my whole life looking into the eyes of anyone and everyone to determine who I was and how I would be. I endured incredible abuse, even at my own hands. But, I finally got to a point where I stood up for myself, against myself, and allowed myself to find a way to love myself unconditionally. Not loving yourself unconditionally is what I believe to be the most important thing in what keeps us from our wonderful life.

As a society, we have come to an understanding that there is a part of us called the Ego. The Toltec called it the Mitote. Although we are not separate from any part of this wonderful and huge Universe, the Ego is an important part of what makes us different from other aspects of it. A tree doesn't care what the tree next to

The Missing Piece in Self-Love

looks like. A bird doesn't take something personal, and hold a grudge for the remainder of its days. You can't be more in the moment than a blade of grass. A moment in time when nothing matters. Everything is just perfect. No judgement, no chaos. Everything just is, allowing everything else to just be. Peaceful, wouldn't you agree? What is it though, about being human that keeps us out of that way of thought? The Ego. The Ego is a part of our mind that works around the clock helping us see the world for what it isn't. Two things you can count on from the Ego is that it never sleeps, and it doesn't understand reality.

We came into this world a perfect being. Through our parents, friends, schools, media, and every other source of education you can think of, we developed over time ideas and judgements that allow us to complete a mathematical equation that gives us an opportunity to understand the world around us. We put thoughts together, allowing them to add up to something we can relate to, based on what we individually collect through time. As a result we pass judgement, take things personally, and ultimately keep ourselves from self-love. Allowing for a virtual playground for drama and chaos.

Believe me, I didn't fall onto this understanding very easily. But when I figured this out, it was the beginning of my own heaven on earth. It was a big "Aha" moment that opened flood gates of processing. Many thoughts came to me. "Sounds easy enough, but how on earth do you live in the world of today and allow this information to exist?" "How am I able to step outside of my own little private box and disconnect from my Ego?"

The truth is that you can't disconnect from your Ego. It is a part of you that will always be there, and will always be doing exactly what it is meant to do. That is to try and keep you stuck in your human self. Not allowing you to really see what beautiful things the universe and your world around you are offering. It keeps you from truly loving yourself unconditionally, and finally giving yourself a chance at the life that you really want. The life that is divinely your birth right. You are meant to have a life as a human, who through unconditional self-love, lives a life of heaven on earth. A life where nothing is failure. A life that allows you the opportunity to grow, and develop in a way that best suits you. Free from chaos, drama, judgement and any other thing that keeps you from being truly happy. A life filled with freedom and peace. Without this freedom you can never truly have happiness. You will not just know, but begin to understand, that what other people say, do or think doesn't make any difference in your life. You begin to understand that each moment in your life doesn't get to dictate who you are, and what your life will be. You will eventually understand how significant it is to live in the moment, like a blade of grass. Allowing each one to go by just as clouds in the sky. Beautiful to look at, but gone. With another coming right behind it. Passing by as a beautiful piece of the world with no real significance. The only significant thing about a moment is what you make of it.

The Ego is what keeps you from being able to be in that place. Yes, your thoughts are what builds your dreams. They are what helps you go from one moment to the next, but you don't have to be attached to them. Dreams are perfectly healthy, and you should live out your dreams. However life has this crazy way of throwing curve balls at you. You can't help what someone or something does along the way that can change everything in your perfect plan. Not allowing you to develop your dreams into expectations, will allow you to be free from distractions and curve balls getting in the way. Causing a sense of disappointment and failure.

Learn to be honest with yourself. Honesty in what we say and do is very important, but there is nothing more important about

The Missing Piece in Self-Love

honesty than giving it to yourself. You will be giving yourself a chance to get to know YOU better.

Learn to respect your emotions. Your emotions are a part of you that makes you the beautiful person that you are. Your feelings though, you should keep aware of, because your feelings are nothing more than a development of thoughts you have as a result of the egoist part of your mind.

Learn to not take things personally. Don't have attachments to events. Don't have attachments to what others say and do. This only builds a platform for self-judgement. Which is one the worst things you can do to yourself. You came into this world perfect, and that is what you still are.

Remember that it is nice to dream, but don't allow that dream to result in expectations. They will only set you up for a life that is less than happy.

Be good to yourself. Remember that each and every day you will have less, or more, to offer than another day in your life, and that's ok. Don't beat yourself up if you have less in you today. Be honest with yourself about what you have to offer and present yourself with honesty, giving just that.

Let the past be in the past. Memories may serve you, but being attached to them won't. They are frozen in time, and so is that part of you in that moment. Passed by like the clouds in the sky.

When dealing with something becomes difficult, ask yourself what it is that you fear. Realize that fear is the emotion triggered by thoughts you accept as being real.

Respect your journey, and the journey of others. They too are doing what they can with what they have to build their own heaven on earth. Without judgement on others, you diminish your judgement on yourself, allowing for everything to go on as it should.

These are a few of the things you can adopt in your life that will encourage you to love yourself better, giving you the life that you want. Filled with freedom and love. However, there is still one more thing that is the most important of all.

Remember that you are human. You will, from time to time, fall from one or all of these. Respect that you are human and that this will happen. Because it will, over and over again. Give yourself a chance to let go of it, and move on with great love for yourself. You are honestly the one person that will ever understand you, and love you, more than anyone else can. Allow it to happen, and enjoy what is reality. That you are a perfect human being.

The Missing Piece in Self-Love

Letisha Galloway

Letisha Galloway is an international bestselling author, book coach, poet, and speaker. She is the co-author of When New Life Begins, Family Ties: What Binds Us and Tears Us Apart, The Missing Piece: A Life Transformed, and The Missing Piece in Forgiveness. Letisha authored a book titled Victim to Victor: A Story of Love, Failure and Faith which chronicles her life as an abandoned child, domestic violence survivor, losing her only child, and many other life changing events. Letisha is regularly involved in bringing awareness to domestic violence. Letisha is active in child abuse prevention activities. Additionally Letisha advocates for the homeless and ending hunger.

You can reach Letisha at:

Email:
letisha.nicole@gmail.com

Website:
www.letisha.galloway.com

Facebook:
https://www.facebook.com/authorletishagalloway

Compiled By Kate Gardner

Twitter:
https://twitter.com/letisha_nicole

LinkedIn:
https://www.linkedin.com/profile/view?id=239265016&trk=nav_responsive_tab_profile

The Missing Piece in Self-Love

Beautifully Broken
By Letisha Galloway

"I'm sorry I didn't mean for this to happen she's pregnant", he said. At the very moment that my 17 year old boyfriend uttered those words my 14 year old heart was shattered. My boyfriend (who I was limited in seeing) had gotten another person pregnant while he was on summer vacation. As I looked at the phone in disbelief tears began to stream down my face. He didn't even have the decency to tell me face to face. I didn't understand how someone who claimed to love me could betray me in such a major way. He apologized numerous times and I took him back, only for him to betray me again. I accepted the betrayal because I was insecure. I didn't think that anyone else wanted me. I had deep rooted insecurities.

My insecurities were not obvious, because I hid them behind smiles and laughter. My legs were amputated when I was a baby. Being an amputee didn't always trouble me but it did when it came to dating. I always wondered if I was good enough. I was one of the last of my friends to get a boyfriend and I thought that I should hold on to him at any cost, even my self-respect. I eventually ended the relationship but the dysfunction would continue. My first romantic relationship set the stage for my many other dysfunctional relationships later on.

When I was 17 and was able to experience more freedom, I became involved in an abusive relationship. My 20 year old boyfriend told me that he loved me and, I wanted to hear that. He was the answer to all of my dreams but my dreams were slowly shattering into pieces. He first hit me a year into the relationship.

I kept coming back because he said he was sorry and he loved me. I made excuses for him and declared that the abuse was my fault. My reasoning at that age was that no one would hit you unless you did something wrong, or insulted them. I didn't realize that no matter what words are said, no one has the right to physically assault you. I accepted the abuse because I didn't know how to love myself. I thought that if I could just do what he said he would love me enough to stop hitting me. I thought I could change him but I didn't realize that I needed to change myself.

After I left the abusive relationship I continued searching for someone to love me. I got involved in one bad relationship after the other. My selection process for romantic partners was not very selective at all. I didn't have any standards. If I was at a party and you had a pulse, and said I was pretty you were my new boyfriend. I didn't care about getting to know a person before getting involved. I just wanted someone to love me. I continued the party life and entered one destructive and dysfunctional relationship after the other for several years. It was a vicious cycle. The true love that I was looking for escaped me. I failed to realize that the love I was chasing after would continue to escape me, because I hadn't learned to love myself. I kept attracting men who wouldn't love me either. I still continued on in my search for love.

As soon as one relationship ended I entered into another. The new relationship would take place weeks to a few months after my last relationship ended. On a few occasions I found someone else within days of my previous relationship ending. In my mind I convinced myself that I was simply moving on but, in reality, I was hiding my pain and insecurities behind the new relationship. I didn't allow myself time to heal from the previous relationship. I would take the pain and hurt from the previous relationship, and enter into a new one. The new relationship was like a band aid that sealed the hurt from the previous experience temporarily.

The Missing Piece in Self-Love

As good as band aids are they all eventually fall off. Allowing sufficient time to heal from a relationship is important. When a relationship ends, time should be taken for self-reflection. The end of the relationship is not the time to go immediately searching for new love. The desperation for love has the ability to cloud judgment when screening potential mates.

Learning to love yourself is not an easy process for most people. We are our harshest critics. Most people always find a reason to criticize themselves about some area they feel they lack in whether it is hair, weight, social status, etc. The important thing to remember is that everyone has flaws. It is easy and tempting to look at another person and become envious because it seems that they have it all together. Appearances can be deceiving because we are all people and struggle with some form of insecurity, whether we admit it to ourselves or not.

In order to love yourself a change in mindset is needed. When you have a negative thought, learn to change it into a positive thought. One of my common negative thoughts was that I was not worthy of a good man and nobody will love me. I had to change my mindset and start telling myself that I am beautiful, I am worthy, and that someone, someday, will be happy to have me as a partner. When I changed my mindset my perception of myself changed. Today I am a single lady patiently waiting on my mate to find me. I'm not looking. I am taking time discover more about myself. When my mate does find me I will be able to compliment his life because I am no longer desperate and broken. Although my dysfunctional relationships were painful to go through, they taught me valuable lessons about self-love. Here are some things that I learned about self-love and relationships.

Compiled By Kate Gardner

God First

My faith was an important part of me learning to love myself. God does not make mistakes. I came to the realization that God created me exactly how he wanted. He creates beautiful things. I learned to see myself as beautiful even with my flaws. We all have flaws. It is the flaws that make us unique. No one is perfect and trying to be perfect will cause frustration and disappointment. Accept who you are because you are beautiful. When you learn to accept that you are beautiful you value yourself and no relationship will be able to devalue you. When you recognize that God loves you, anything less than love is unacceptable in a relationship. When you pray you are able to get revelation from God about potential mates. It works for me. He has revealed to me many times spiritually that potential mates are not a good fit for me and I listened.

Respect Yourself

Everyone is worthy of love and respect. Past mistakes do not matter when it comes to the respect. We are all God's creations and no one person is better or more important than the other. Respecting yourself is important if you expect others to do the same. Carrying yourself with dignity and class is key to self-love. A part of loving yourself is not allowing anyone to bring you out of character. During a conversation, a person may disrespect you and it may be hard to hold your peace, but try stay true to respecting yourself and not go down to their level. When you love yourself people's opinions of you do not have a great impact on your self-image. A potential partner will see that you respect yourself and either follow suit or walk away, either way it's a blessing. If your partner respects you then a relationship can be built out of mutual respect. If the potential mate does not choose to respect you and they walk away it is good because a mate with no respect for you is not desirable.

Set Boundaries

People will treat you how you allow them to treat you. You can speak and let people know how to treat you in a classy manner. It's acceptable to let people know that they shouldn't be speaking to you in certain tones or with certain words. If they continue to ignore your wishes then you have every right to move on in life without them. You have the right to set boundaries. Don't let anyone make you feel guilty for setting boundaries. If you do not set healthy boundaries some people will take advantage and treat you badly over a long period of time. When you set boundaries it shows people that you value yourself. When you value yourself, others will begin to see the value in you.

The journey to self-love is not easy, but it is needed. Loving yourself causes your inner light to shine brightly in a world that is often filled with darkness. Continue to shine brightly.

Compiled By Kate Gardner

Lisa Beane

Lisa Beane, International Best Selling Published Author and Certified Integrative Nutrition Health Coach.

Lisa's story of ill health and mandatory behavior change at 46 were the inspiration in forming BeaneNATURAL. She bridges the gap between traditional medicine and holistic health via lifestyle intervention.

Through Lisa's guidance you'll learn to open up your mind and find clarity in seeing your possibilities; to which are the solutions you have within you.

Walking away with improved confidence, you will be empowered to become the healthiest, happiest and best version of you.

Lisa's work globally includes:

Coaching Virtual/Live Retreats Speaking Engagements

Motivational/Educational Workshops

You can reach Lisa at:

Email:
lisa@beanenatural.com

Facebook:
www.facebook.com/lisa.a.beane

Website:
http://beanenatural.com

LinkedIn:
https://www.linkedin.com/pub/lisa-beane/19/122/325

Compiled By Kate Gardner

What's Love Got to Do With It?
By Lisa Beane

It was a beautiful day when I was asked to help a person, organization or a business. Why, yes! Of course, I can do that for you! I truly enjoyed doing for others. By being a giver of my time, energy, and attention, I was helping, which flattered me. My thought process changed when I lost my health and vitality, my adrenals were blown, I was in pain all over and I couldn't get out of bed.

Finally, I threw in the towel, quit my job and decided to find a better way. I never once questioned the impact quitting my job would have on my family or me, as I had no quality of life to speak of. My husband was my driving force, as he said, "quit!" "We will figure it out. You have been burning the candle at both ends far too long and you have one foot in the grave at the age of 47," said by a Holistic Practitioner! My reserves were shot and I couldn't go on another day, with nothing left to give.

This is the journey and lifestyle I created. Why you might ask? I did it because I was a "yes" person and couldn't say "no!" I did it because I was a perfectionist and didn't know what it meant to honor me with self-love. Honestly, I didn't know I was to love myself first and foremost. I thought I was supposed to be there for everyone else and *if* there was time to take care of me, I would! If not, I would go without an adequate amount of sleep or the proper nutrition as I went to all ends of the earth for my family, friends, career and organizations.

The Missing Piece in Self-Love

It took me becoming extremely ill to take a step back and re-evaluate the way I lived my life. The stress in my life, the foods I ate, and how I had the need to control everything around me was *not* my friend. It took me looking at my health, relationships and my career, to decide that I loved myself enough to make a change. This change would come with a big price. My career came with a large client database within a 200-mile radius, representatives and a desirable paycheck. By visiting that database often, the *company* would have an amazing retention rate and I would receive decent compensation.

It is important to learn from our experiences and mistakes. I believe, in fact, this was my destiny so that I could be provoked enough to repair and rejuvenate my total being. I *finally* loved myself enough to get out of my own way, push past my fears and learn when to call it quits. I left the security of my career of 10 years, just like that.

When I took a step forward in my new journey, I knew there was no turning back. I was being guided by God, and by the people who were showing up in my life. I had become open minded, aware and awake enough to know that I must do the work for myself, not for anyone else this time.

Self-love is about nurturing yourself with respect and kindness, so that you have something left to give to others, without using up your last bit of reserves. It is about being where you want to be or at least working toward what makes you happy and makes your heart sing. If you're in a situation at home, work or around your tribe of which you have relationships with and you have a heavy heart, listen to what that sounds like, and feel what that feels like. It could be your body's way of speaking to you. How do you feel when you are in relationships and they are on-again, off-again? One minute all is good, but with a flip of a switch, it is no longer good. Are these relationships putting you into a bad mood, making you grumpy or making you question your decisions? If so, know that it is your body's way of recognizing something isn't right for you. It's essential that we listen to our body. Our body speaks to us. Although we are conditioned, to ignore the signs, we feel the need to be in charge.

I can say that when my health began to improve, holistically, I felt the need to shout out to the world and wanted to help people take their control back. I wanted to let people know they don't have to settle for ill health, poor relationships, and lack of self-love. I would say that when one begins to heal their gut, decides to make the right food choices, and creates good sleep habits, their mind clears and things begin to make perfect sense.

Some of the ways I have invested in, and deposited into, my self-love account are by listening to music while sipping on a cup of hot lemon water and watching out of my window for the different types of stillness, critters and landscapes each season has to offer. I see a Chiropractor weekly, a massage therapist monthly and I have my nails done. I choose to keep the TV off when home alone, to avoid the negative noise in my head. I do not listen to the news, as it is lacking anything positive and uplifting to report. Coloring mandalas to beautiful and soulful music is a fun and therapeutic way to relax. Rebounding and walking are my favorite types of movement. I have learned to enjoy myself and love myself enough to know when to avoid certain situations that do not serve me. I thrive on surrounding myself with like-minded people. I oil pull, dry brush, juice, blend, cook with music and love to read things that make me laugh. I spend quality time with my family and make time for my friends. I have learned to work in my home office without music, most days, depending on what I am working on and how much train of thought I need. I take time away by myself, even if it is just a drive around town. I travel, not

The Missing Piece in Self-Love

always far, but I do get away. There is something so therapeutic about being in a car with the music on, sunroof and windows open while the car cruises along with the wind blowing in my hair. I now understand where my son gets his love for *cruising*. Although I am very alert and oriented, driving in this manner gives me the ability to decompress and helps clear my mind. It doesn't bother me a bit to go into a restaurant or business by myself. Since my health declined, I struggle with a lot of commotion in my brain, so I need to do these things to help my sanity and to gain clarity. It is imperative that I get to the beach as often as I can to catch the beautiful sunsets, walk on the sand, feed my body with Vitamin D, and be in the salty air and ocean.

I re-gained my passion for life. I stopped letting fear stand in my way. So what if I tried something and I failed at it. It wouldn't hurt me or make me less of an individual. All it could really do is make me a stronger person by picking myself up by my panties and trying again. Through this adventure, I repaired a broken marriage and this journey allowed me to have nourishing relationships with others, again.

It is important for me to share my life in hopes to touch other people's lives. I no longer wanted my story, or myself, to be the world's best kept secret. Therefore, I became an Integrative Nutrition Health Coach and have built my brand and mission around my joy.

I would like to leave you with this.

It has been quite the journey, and a journey is truly what it is. We all have different ambitions, goals, feelings, issues and thoughts. I ask that each of you reading this, be encouraged enough to do the necessary work to create your own amount of self-love.

Self-love is about setting boundaries. It's about being able to say no. It's about caring for, and taking responsibility for, oneself. It is about respecting and trusting oneself and not needing to be dependent on anyone for approval. We cannot truly love another until we truly love ourselves. Self-love is about being mindful. It's about acting on our needs verses our wants. In order to practice self-love, one must practice good self-care. It's about protecting and forgiving oneself. Self-love is also about being true and authentic to you!

Know we were designed to have beautiful and bountiful lives, as long as we are able to recognize it and live life accordingly. Live intentionally, on purpose and out loud.

What is your missing piece in self-love?

The Missing Piece in Self-Love

Lori Blake-Leighton

Lori is a best-selling international co-author in the book, 'The Missing Piece: A Transformational Journey.'

She resides in Washington state with her husband of 25 years and together they have a son and granddaughter.

Her life is full of passion and beauty, as she loves to paint and connect her community with other local artists.

Lori was the co-host for the radio show, 'Women of Wisdom' and has the Facebook community, 'In the Company of Women.'

"This book is dedicated to Shane, Zack and Dakota for showing me what true love is."

You can reach Lori at:

Facebook:
Author Lori Kay Blake-Leighton

Facebook:
From The Heart

Facebook:
In The Company Of Women

Compiled By Kate Gardner

Email:
lkblake.64@gmail.com

Self-Love: The Art of Acceptance
By Lori Blake-Leighton

Most people usually view self-love in much the same way; 7-8 hours of sleep, eat healthy, drink plenty of water, exercise, soak in a bubble bath, etc., but there is more to it than that. It can also be an emotional, spiritual, social and global experience.

It may dwell in being connected to Mother Earth, her refreshing cool waters, her majestic mountains, her fragrant lush plant life and her fierce but fragile animal kingdom. Or gazing up at Father Universe and seeing the beautiful azure sky, images in the cotton ball clouds, or the pink and orange painted sunrise in the morning and the distant moon with its glittering diamond stars at night.

Maybe it is smiling at passing strangers, paying it forward at a coffee shop or saying "Thank You" to a Veteran. Making googly eyes to comfort a crying child, taking in a stray cat or helping someone on the side of the road...all of these acts require empathy and compassion. These are just a few colors of self-love that create pleasure and satisfaction within ourselves.

Speaking our truth (the words in our heart, the emotions from our soul) is the first step in self-love. It creates the pallet to which all other colors of our life will be available to us. When we are truthful about ourselves we create an image, a portrait that will be forever imprinted in our mind and in the minds of others.

Loving our self is a journey to which there is no end. It is a daily practice, a transformation that we must surrender to and know that by doing so, it will lead us down paths to healthier and more vibrant adventures.

Learning who we are as individuals is an art form in itself. It is an educational facility where we are both the teacher AND the student. We see the world around us and chose the colors that work best for our own creation. Sometimes we mix emotions that make our view murky, but they can always be corrected.

In this ever changing learning environment, we also gain knowledge from the mistakes of others, as well as our own. We need to listen to the wisdom that a good friend, spiritual advisor or motivational speaker may offer because they have learned new ways to create self-love.

Knowing the value (shadow and light) is key to balance in our lives. It is very important to have gratitude for the unpleasant times as well as the good, because the darker days usually have a lesson in them...a lesson we can choose to chalk up to wisdom. The choices we make are part of self-awareness. In order for us to love ourselves, certain choices need to be made to ensure our happiness and really, that is what self-love is...happiness.

Putting ourselves first is imperative. We hear it every time we are on a flight, "put the oxygen mask on yourself first before helping others." Why? We cannot be of much assistance to others if we have passed out! It is the same in our daily lives. It is essential that we regard ourselves as significant...that we should come first. If we are healthy in mind, body and spirit because we have chosen to put ourselves as the highest priority, then the path is clear to create beauty and joy in our lives. This is considered part of the law of attraction. What we put out will come back. Our own self-love affects everyone around us.

The Missing Piece in Self-Love

The evolution of our body of work will have many titles. Woman in particular have titles ranging from Mama Bear, to Queen of Fools, to Goddess Warrior. Some have traversed many muddy ditches in the hopes of helping loved ones get on their feet and connect them to their own self-love but sometimes to the detriment of themselves and others around them. We forget to stand in the light of our own self-care before extending our hand to help others see their own worth.

It is extremely important that our intentions have clarity when trying to honor ourselves or others. By honoring ourselves, we give permission to set healthy boundaries so that we may give AND receive and if we trust ourselves, others will see the greatness within us. When that happens, we are illuminated. It is a radiant glow that can be seen in our eyes, heard in our voice and felt through our touch. Artistry at its finest.

Self-love is a very powerful, sacred act and emotion. Like pigment in paint, it is embedded in the conscious and subconscious parts of our mind but it needs to be used constantly to keep it malleable. It is a positive vibration that can heal us. It speaks a language that our mind, body and soul understands. The vibration frequency of self-love cannot be heard by the ear but it can be felt by the heart.

We have many breakthroughs while learning to love ourselves and are reminded constantly to be still, to breathe, to look around and see what obstacle is in our path and remove it, or at least go around it. These breakthroughs can be rough and sharp around the edges. They can be painful like slivers but feel better after being pulled out and dealt with. We learn that with self-love, comes self-acceptance.

Accepting one's self is not always easy. Like any artist, we are our own worst critic. We tend to shy away from complements and steer clear from spot lights that may be thrown in our direction but in reality, these are beautiful gifts of love from others that we should receive with gratitude. These gifts are from people that appreciate, praise and care about us, and we need to realize our own self-worth. Surrounding ourselves with the most positive people and circumstances ensures that we will have the highest internal and EXTERNAL vibration. The higher the vibration, the better we feel and more the beautiful our environments become.

Another very important part of loving one's self is forgiveness. This means not only forgiveness of others, but of ourselves as well. Holding on to anger, sadness or resentment is very destructive and stagnates our soul. They are very strong emotions, but if we let go of the past and nourish our spirit in the present, love will always win the battle.

We all need down time...to be unplugged from the world. Technology has gobbled up our precious time, but a lot of it is by choice. We need to remember that our choices are what create our reality. Choose to step away from devices and televisions. They require our mental energy and take us away from loved ones and our irreplaceable moments.

We are also swimming in STUFF! The tiny house movement has been all the rage lately and it may not be for everyone but LIVING with less should be. Let's purge our homes, our garages, our offices of excess clutter and make room for the manifestation of individuality and creativity. Materialistic items take time away from our families and ourselves. How many plastic bowls with no lids do we need? Our time is priceless and should take precedence over cleaning closets and the hoarding of non-essential items.

Doing something we enjoy is a great expression of self-love and creates mood enhancing changes. It releases endorphins, which make us feel more positive and give us that "I can do anything" state of mind. Staying clear from the soap opera of others is also a

The Missing Piece in Self-Love

wonderful method to continue to be happy and loving toward ourselves.

Another great way to express that we care about ourselves is to have a moment, a day or even a weekend just for "me". Having me-time is key to unwinding and opening up our essence to more possibilities that the world has to offer. It gives us time to appreciate what we have, and who we are. This is quality time to replenish our energy and our zest for life! This is also a sacred time of self-discovery and once again...acceptance.

Finding ways to love ourselves is different for everyone. Some may feel that self-love seems greedy but it is actually the opposite and is beneficial to our growth. With each brush stroke of love, the beautiful vibrant painting of our life comes into view. It is the COLORS we choose that will make the difference.

Like all artwork, not everyone agrees on the beauty that a piece may hold but the only opinion of acceptance that matters for each individual canvas, is from the artists' themselves.

Compiled By Kate Gardner

Lynn Jones

Lynn is a woman of courage, who inspires others with her amazing life story. Her health and life collapsed after being harmed by the medical profession, but transformed by becoming an expert in self-help. Suffering has led to a wealth of understanding on the nature of abuse and the healing power of love.

Through self-directed learning, Lynn works to promote a better and safer way of working for medical students. Through writing and speaking, Lynn works to reduce abuse, promote love and empower people to redress the balance of power. Lynn is a life coach, helping personal growth and change.

You can reach Lynn at:

E-mail:
jones_m_lynn@hotmail.com

From Brokenness to Wholeness

By Lynn Jones

As I look back over my life, it seems a miracle I have survived, an even greater miracle to come through richer for the experience, and a huge relief to be moving towards enlightenment.

My journey from self-hate to self-love has been like a long and arduous marathon. I have spent the summer of my life working to overcome trauma from my early life and emotional problems that mostly stemmed back to my relationship with Patsy, my sister.

Patsy was 3½ years old at the time of my birth, which is known to be the worst age for jealousy. With dad away at war, she spent the first year and a half her life living with my mother and maternal grandmother. My earliest memory of Patsy was her chant that she repeated over and over again 'I hate our dad, I wish he was dead and it was just me, my mum and my gran'. There was no place for me in her life.

With exclusion as the female form of bullying, Patsy worked to push me out from the time I was born until her death a year ago, with an ongoing theme of using my display of distress to justify her behaviour. When I did challenge Patsy for the way she treated me, her response was 'I do this because of no fault of my own, but because you are a horrible person'.

I was a vulnerable child and suffered three types of sexual abuse, outside the family. As I was too young to know the facts of life, the abuse meant nothing to me at the time, but lay dormant in the repressed memory.

Compiled By Kate Gardner

My mother was timid, teaching me to believe in authority figures and defer to their superior knowledge. She constantly told me 'be good, be good', but never told me what she wanted or affirmed my goodness. I have spent my life seeking definition of what it is to be good, which started as an infant, looking to the church and the example of Jesus. I became the only church goer in the family and developed spiritual and moral values, in line with church teaching.

With full trust in the medical profession, I suffered a terrifying ordeal after a doctor promised sedation for a phobia at the time of giving birth and then went back on his word. I suffered psychosis as a result, and my greatest fear has been that doctors could take things out of my hands, it could happen all over again, and I would be re-abused. Survival has depended on searching my soul to understand what had gone wrong, with a desperate need to be heard and understood.

The saying 'when the pupil is ready the teacher will appear' has proved true for me. At a university meeting, at the age of 60, I made friends with Rae Gingell, who is an astrologer and counselling psychologist. After some time listening to stories of sexual abuse in childhood, medical abuse, disastrous relationships with doctors and the collapse of my life and health, she put it to me that I had Aspergers. I cried. After years of trying to recover from a character assassination from my ex-husband, who denied paternity at the time of giving birth, and inappropriate mental health labels, Aspergers rang true and it felt there was something wrong with me after all.

Rae explained that High Functioning Aspergers meant that I was mildly autistic, wired differently from the average person and that people with Aspergers look out of a different window on the world. Information is taken in and processed differently, resulting in different conclusions.

The Missing Piece in Self-Love

I have been misunderstood from birth, and my life was like a ship that started off 1 degree off course at the beginning of my life journey, and ended up hundreds of miles out of true by the end. With Aspergers as a point of reference, I was able to make better sense of my world and get life back on course.

As a feminist, Rae taught me about patriarchal ideology, and why the way I believed life ought to be was a false premise. I had always felt that I was a let-down, but started to see that I had been let down by the system. Much of my self-loathing was in the belief I had failed, but my life and health collapsed because beliefs inherited from the world failed me and did not hold up when put to the test.

All good things come to an end, and my dear friend moved out of England to be with her family in a remote part of Ireland, where our life-long friendship now relies on posting long winded letters as our means of communication.

A lot of people have told me I am hard on myself. The humiliation from my life experience has been so bad that it has been like having an inner tyrant driving me to prove myself. I take pride in being a lifelong learner, with great satisfaction that through self-directed learning, I moved from being a non-thinking person to becoming an intellectual. In the past ten years I have qualified as a life-coach and lectured to student nurses on therapeutic relationships and to student doctors on how to spot Aspergers. Evaluation results have been very encouraging and trainee doctors ask 'Why haven't we been taught this?'

I met Jackie Hawken at her workshops on life coaching and Buddhism. With great interest in healing through spiritual perspective, I asked to have 1:1 sessions with her to accept, allow, and release difficult feelings. To my delight I found Jackie is a psychological coach with knowledge of female Aspergers. As a clinical psychologist, she confirmed Aspergers and was keen to understand why I had a recurring pattern of exclusion running through my life.

Jackie was able to identify that my default in life was 'scapegoat'. I could see the recurring theme in my family, the in-laws and in certain work roles. As scapegoat, this enabled others to put negative responsibility on to me, while denying me my own positive personal power. One of the major factors in personality disorder is denying any part in the problem. There is a recurring theme throughout my life, as I look to those who have used me as scapegoat. Jackie was also able to see my part in the dysfunction, which enabled me to make changes. I am now able to accept that I am who I am, life is as it is, others are who they are and on their own journey.

I have found there is ignorance around Aspergers, especially with the medical profession, where certain behaviours that are normal coping strategies become diagnosed as mental health problems. One example is feelings cannot be dealt with at gut level, so go through the intellect, which is exhausting. This spills out into writing as a safety valve, but puts a tick in the mental health box.

Like everyone else, I built my world on beliefs and mine broke down following medical abuse.

I have gone deep within myself, and studied spirituality and social sciences to find answers. With greater self-respect and trust in myself, I am now better at owning my own power.

My most recent mentor has been Nicky Marshall. I have worked my way through the Discover Your Bounce programme with her guidance. This programme has empowered me to create my own vision of my life, with goals to aim for and easy techniques to sustain resilience, daily health and wellbeing. Together we have tracked my progress, from being able to 'bounce back' from challenges to fulfilling my dream of becoming a writer

The Missing Piece in Self-Love

My journey has been one from brokenness to wholeness. In my early years, life ran true to my family script, but when the bottom fell out of my world, I suffered what I described as dislocation of the soul. My false-self had collapsed and I was running out of true.

I set out to understand the meaning of life and search for truth and life purpose. Spirituality was my point of reference with integrity as my yard stick to test the truths. The saying 'truth isn't because something is added, but because something is taken away' has proved true for me. Often, when beliefs broke down it felt like earth tremors to my belief system, but it was in taking away false beliefs from my own interpretation or inherited that I was able to align and connect to true-self.

In making the move to wholeness, there has been a healthy shift to self, where I have forgiven myself for not being able to get it right and am happy with who I am and the life purpose that is unfolding.

At the age of 67, my future looks bright. Having learned from the lessons of the past, my intention is to move beyond teaching at university to sharing with the wider community through writing, speaking and life coaching.

My advice to readers is to believe in you, and form a strong personal foundation. Through self-awareness, self-respect and, most importantly self-love, you can live the life you love and love the life you live

Compiled By Kate Gardner

Matthew Cipes

Matthew Cipes is a Registered Massage Therapist in Kelowna, B.C. Canada, a Martial Arts Instructor, Wholistic Health and Wellness Coach, and Global Networker. He is passionate about philanthropy, living a healthy lifestyle, personal development and empowerment of self and others. He loves helping individuals find their vision to joyfully move forward in their lives with clarity and balance in order to have significant physical, financial and personal breakthroughs along the way. Connect with Matthew through Facebook, LinkedIn or via email at mdcipes@gmail.com to advance in your journey, to learn the tools and skills necessary to transform your life in a healthy positive way, and to experience greater fulfilment, freedom, happiness, and abundance in all areas of your life.

You can reach Matthew at:

Email:
mdcipes@gmail.com

From Breakdown Comes Breakthrough
By Matthew Cipes

It was a beautiful sunny afternoon, as I peddled toward a very busy street beyond a blind corner...suddenly an oncoming blur, a loud THUD...feeling handlebars whipping out of my grasp, with the distinct sounds of metal denting, twisting and clanking against the pavement with a screech of tires as I flew from the now mangled bike and landed hard on the road. "What happened?" I thought..."I just crashed into the driver's door of a fast moving car, and...I'm alright!" Before that shocking childhood moment, I longed for the emotional pain to stop. I was carelessly acting out, being reckless, and flirting with death. I had just experienced a turning point, a major life changing moment, and had realized that yes, I was very happy to be alive!

Much of my young life has been very difficult, full of challenge and intense heartache, beginning before Grade 1, and continuing into Grade 10. Perhaps because I was short, scrawny, spoke with a lisp, and had various nervous tics, I was mercilessly and relentless bullied, teased, shoved, tripped, punched, kicked, criticized, laughed at and ridiculed. The more I cried, yelled, pleaded and begged for it to stop, the worse it got. I was regularly targeted by kids with rocks, spit balls, or garbage, called demeaning names, threatened, or had cruel jokes played on me. I began to believe them after a while, became hyper critical as I compared myself to others, and began to lose all hope, joy and self-confidence. Wishing to be "normal", to fit in and to be more like the other kids, I felt shut down, highly introverted and didn't like who I was.

Compiled By Kate Gardner

I'm not expressing this to gain sympathy or empathy, and don't want you to hold any anger or ill will toward those people. I've already given them enough precious time and energy, so please forgive, and let it go. My intention is to encourage growth, and let you know that you're not alone. As we learn new skills, we change our beliefs, so I chose to forgive those individuals, and also forgave myself for allowing myself to believe them, take it personally and become so hurt in the process.

Life improved in high school by earning the respect of my peers through skateboarding. In the skating culture, if you're not coming home bashed, bruised, bumped, broken, bonked or bleeding, then you're simply not pushing yourself enough. After a good skate session, we'd brag to each other about our scrapes and mishaps, laugh at our ratty home-repaired torn shoes, clothing, and equipment, and discuss new "rad" moves. We felt like Kings, respected each other, and pushed ourselves every day to advance. The more often and harder we fell, the more determined we were to get back up! I was a passionate member of my high school skate club in New York, so when I moved to B.C. Canada for Grade 11, I immediately took a bold risk, suppressed my shyness and went to speak with the Vice Principal. We successfully initiated a new skate club, when previously, skateboards weren't even allowed on school property! Although it was strange at first, I enjoyed my newfound popularity, and embraced my inner weirdo! I often wore unmatched colored socks with two different shoes, and cruised down the hallways walking on my hands. I continued skating, learning martial arts, started snowboarding and drumming, and soon joined a rock band!

Hey, life doesn't happen to us, it happens FOR us!! We are 100% responsible for our own thoughts, mindset and decisions. We are all connected, and act as mirrors for each other, so whatever we

The Missing Piece in Self-Love

judge in others, we judge within ourselves. We tend to grow strong only when we're challenged, similar to a young tree. If we're overly sheltered, and don't have the elements beating on us, then our roots won't be stimulated to grow deep, robust and resilient. We improve as we live through the lightning storms, heavy wind, driving rain, drought, and the occasional brush with creatures. Events happen in life, and we choose how to respond based on our experience, wisdom, skill level and mindset. Sometimes we are the victims of an event, but we choose whether to remain a victim in fear and lack, or to move forward with abundance as a leader.

I chose to grow through it instead of just go through it. I aspired to transmute the pain as an alchemist, and shape pearls as an Oyster does with irritating grains of sand. I chose to turn my test into a testimony, and devoted my life to serving others, to draw from my experience to help empower others to transcend their limiting beliefs. Everything we say, think, believe and do is a skill. Any skill can be learned through discipline, commitment, dedication, practice, following proven method, and having willingness to breakdown or fail, then evaluate our experience afterwards to grow stronger in balance.

No one is above or better than anyone else. We all have different mountains to climb, and that's all part of the journey. Nobody's perfect, we all make mistakes and will all fail sometimes, so don't ever give up on you, or your dreams! The more we fail, the quicker we learn! Sometimes people seem to go out of their way to overthink things, stray from the path, create drama, distraction, and partake in many forms of self-medication. These may include heavy drinking, recreational drug use, addictions, unhealthy obsessions (such as bullying), over eating, extensive television or video gaming, relationship hopping...anything done in excess to hide out and avoid the pain of facing the life that they have co-created; or because they simply cannot yet take full responsibility and face the fact that they may not be doing all that they are capable of in life. We've all been there, myself included, stuck in one way or another, and we all have the choice to visit, or to remain there. It's disturbing to realize that we may have lost or forgotten our dreams and passion for life. It can create bitterness, anger, and frustration, selfishly lashing out, teasing, or snapping at other people, sometimes pushing away those we love or admire. Hmmm... Perhaps it's a good reminder that we can't change anyone else, we can only change ourselves, lead by example, be an inspiration through our actions, and empower others with optimism that they will change themselves.

Everyone is unique, special, beautiful, and a leader in his or her own way. Recognizing the need for personal growth is a sign of great strength and is to be celebrated!! It takes courage to face our limiting beliefs that don't serve us, that overly critical voice in our head, and move forward while still feeling fear. I'm full of gratitude for the encouragement of friends, family, mentors, coaches and positive supportive community! The more I learn and grow, the more empowered, creative, giving, loving, peaceful, and at ease with the world I feel. I've begun to understand the missing piece, and feel unconditional love at last. I love myself, life, and appreciate all of the beautiful lessons and teachers along the way! Thank you.

As a loving father of two wonderful girls, I continue to devote myself to becoming a better man, being in service to others, honor and embrace spirituality, and seek universal truth. I trained as a Registered Massage Therapist, Martial Arts Instructor, studied Holistic Nutrition, Health and Wellness Coaching, and continue my journey of self-development, leadership coaching, contribution and significance. I credit Martial Arts philosophy to consistently strive to become a master, have respect, integrity,

The Missing Piece in Self-Love

eternal optimism, take risks, set goals, consciously persevere to improve and hone our skills, and assist others.

What's self-love? It goes far beyond the regard for one's own well-being and happiness. It's having the respect, appreciation, self-worth, integrity, authenticity and acceptance of our whole selves just as we are now, with all of our mistakes, quirks, flaws, and imperfections. By nature, it isn't narcissistic, but is a very desirable trait, that encompasses proper self-care, rest, sleep, nutrition, exercise, positive self-talk, healthy boundaries, capacity for compassion, forgiveness and gratitude, following our gut or intuition, making time for doing what we enjoy, being comfortable in solitude, choosing quality positive likeminded people to be around, taking full responsibility for our own mindset and emotional state, and allowing ourselves to dream BIGGER and go for it! The larger our capacity for self-love, the less of a victim we are, and the more abundant we become, increasing our capability to unconditionally love others. As our mindset improves, so do our feelings making it easier to move forward in life because we make better decisions, have better thoughts, and do better actions.

I've found that being "normal" is severely over-rated, and that all the coolest, most interesting, brilliant, creative, artistic, fun, abundant, free thinking people in the world aren't normal. They stand out because they express their unique differences, live outside the box, and lead by example. They challenge and influence our beliefs and the world as we know it, and we're all good with that.

Compiled By Kate Gardner

Maxine Browne

Maxine Browne contributed a chapter to *The Missing Piece* and *The Missing Piece in Business, The Missing Piece in Forgiveness* and *The Missing Piece in Self-Love,* all of which hit the Amazon Best Seller List. She is the author of *Cinderella's a Fella: He's Nobody's Princess,* as well as *Years of Tears: One Family's Journey Through Domestic Violence.*

Maxine is a book coach. She helps people turn their stories into books. If you have always wanted to write a book, please contact Maxine for a free 30 minute consultation.

You can reach Maxine at:

E-mail:
maxine@maxinebrowne.com

Website:
www.maxinebrowne.com

Facebook:
www.facebook.com/maxine.browne.792

Twitter:
twitter.com/maxinebrowne

Who Am I?
By Maxine Browne

We are born into the role of daughter or son. If we are lucky, we live with a group of people in a family. Within this unit, we are loved and nurtured, we are fed and clothed. As daughter or son, we are accepted. Our parents teach us what is acceptable and what is not. We learn not to jump on the bed, run in the library or play in the street. Our parents teach us there are rules meant to create an orderly society, and there are consequences for breaking those rules.

We learn to talk and walk. And as we grow, we find our next role, that of sister or brother. Our siblings become our playmates and our rivals. We love them, and there are days when we hate them because they won't leave our things alone or they keep coming into our room. They borrow our favorite toy or clothing and get us into trouble. Sometimes they protect us from the bully on the playground. And most days, we get along.

Another role we find ourselves in is that of friend. We have friends in the neighborhood and friends at school. We ride our bikes together, play ball and share our secrets. And as we grow, we may pull away from our family and spend more and more time with our friends.

Then, we meet our spouse and we adopt the role of wife or husband. With this relationship, we find a new level of intimacy and responsibility. We share our life with our mate in a financial partnership. We purchase a home and fill it with possessions. We purchase cars and perhaps toys that we use to entertain ourselves when we are not working.

And another role is that of employee. Our employment pays for our lifestyle. This is another responsibility and role that helps us create stability for our life. With the money we earn we pay for the house, furniture, cars, food and clothing we need to live.

And then we have children. There may be one, two or three bundles of joy that require love and attention. Now it is our turn to not only provide food and clothing, but to teach our children about not jumping on the bed, running in the library or playing in the street. Now it is our turn to bring up the next generation.

As we add the next role, we cannot leave behind the roles of the past. So, we continue to be a son or daughter, a sibling, a friend and a parent. Now the roles of employee begin to clash with the roles of spouse. We find it difficult to juggle our schedule to maintain a vibrant relationship with our life partner. Spending quality time with our parents and children stretches our patience.

And perhaps marriages fail. We may divorce, remarry, and blend families. We add the roles of ex-wife or ex-husband and step-mother or step-father to the list.

And as life gets increasingly complicated you may begin to feel lost. I know I did. By this time, I had two ex-husbands, blended families and everything that comes with it. I had a baby just as my two oldest children were becoming teenagers. In my 50s, I had a child at home, while the oldest was getting married. Soon there would be grandchildren.

I had been Mommy for 30 years. I couldn't even remember what it was like to only worry about what I wanted to do. There were the errands, laundry, meals, homework and driving. There was remembering to fill out the forms, sign the papers or talk to the teacher. There was the never-ending, "Where's my ..." whatever to answer. And life was going by.

It was at this stage that I left my second marriage. During that marriage, I had been oppressed, silenced and erased. I thought I'd made amazing progress when I left, but this was just the first step in a journey of self-discovery.

That summer, my youngest child alternated weeks with her father and me. I had seven days in a row without children or a husband to care for. Once the house was cleaned and the grass mowed, what was I to do with my free time? I hadn't been alone for 30 years.

In the beginning, I watched **mountains** of movies. My marriage had been repressive, and I hadn't seen many movies during the preceding ten years. I had a lot of catching up to do. So, I watched movies back to back to back. I watched all types of movies, especially some that would have been forbidden to me. For a while, this was therapeutic. But soon I began to feel dissatisfied with my solitary movie binges. The time came when it stopped being fun. I wanted more out of life than sitting at home alone, watching television.

And the questions *Is **this** all there is?* and *Who am I?* came more frequently. What kind of life did I want to have? If I could do anything and go anywhere, what would I choose? Instead of watching a movie about someone else's adventures, perhaps I could have a few of my own! I might have been 50, but I was not dead yet.

This was the beginning of discovering who I was.... not mommy, not sister, not wife, but who Maxine was, independent of my roles.

I asked my therapist how to make friends at this age. I didn't know how to do that. She suggested I find something that sounded like fun and invite someone do it with me. During the outing, we could get to know one another. I began to put this into practice.

I went to some community events, visited a few towns in the area and went on some shopping sprees. Gradually, I made several friends and started enjoying my life.

One day, I bought a book and took myself out to dinner. I was extremely uncomfortable as I entered the restaurant. And for the first 10 minutes, I was convinced everyone was looking at me, asking themselves what that lady was doing sitting alone. But then, I began to settle into the space. The food was great, and the book was entertaining. And I soon forgot about everything else and had a lovely meal. Today, if life requires dining alone, it doesn't bother me at all because I enjoy my own company.

As I continued discovering myself, I chose to spend time with people who treated me well and removed myself from the company of those who didn't. Over time, I became selective about who I spent time with. I only spent time with people who showed me respect. And I tried to provide that same kind of space for others. This was new for me because in the past, I accepted all kinds of behavior. It never occurred to me I had a choice. I learned the saying that you teach people how to treat you. And you can remove yourself from unacceptable behavior. And I began to put these ideas into practice.

I loved to travel and dreamed of returning to Mexico. One evening I mentioned this to a couple of friends. As it turned out, they were planning a trip there and invited me along. On that trip, we did everything we could think of. We snorkeled, rode horses and took a tour of a tequila factory. I was on an adventure of my own, and this was no movie.

After my mother's death, my sister and I went on a trip to visit family. We traveled to Iowa, Colorado and British Columbia. During that trip I decided to write about my abusive marriage to help other families. Upon my return, I wrote my first book, *Years of Tears*.

In order to market the book, I found myself guest blogging and writing articles. And the more I wrote, the more I wanted to write. And the writing took on a life of its own.

I began working with domestic violence survivors, helping them tell their stories. And we began a public speaking group to educate the public about healthy relationships. So, telling stories became an ever larger part of my life.

Today I provide book coaching to those who want to write a book but don't know how. This coaching has blossomed into a business that keeps me talking to people from all over the world.

I wouldn't change a thing about my life's journey. The highs and lows have all been instrumental in my ability to talk to folks from every walk of life.

The roles we carry out in life serve a purpose, but we cannot allow them to become a jungle we lose ourselves in. Remain in touch with yourself. You are worth it.

Compiled By Kate Gardner

Meghan Yates

Meghan is a musician, healer, Inter-Spiritual minister, artist, and writer.

She is a graduate of The Maine College of Art and an ordained minister through The Chaplaincy Institute of Maine. Meghan soulfully and artfully companions others through working one-on-one, leading retreats, teaching art and healing classes, and service projects. She spearheads her band, The Reverie Machine, and is prone to mystic moments, creative obsession and experimenting with contemplative practice.

She is always searching for new ways to create, connect and inspire others.

Meghan recently relocated to Washington State with her husband, Mordechai. They are both delighted to call Washington home.

You can reach Meghan at:

Website:
www.meghan-yates.com
www.meghanyatesandthereveriemachine.com

The Missing Piece in Self-Love

Email:
whimsymim@gmail.com

Compiled By Kate Gardner

Lead By a Whisper
By Meghan Yates

The last few years rocked my soul and altered my life. I entered what mystics call a "Dark Night". It started with my heart having electrical problems, which it hadn't had since adolescence. My guts were wrought with painful chronic anxiety from childhood trauma that resurfaced. I had a miscarriage, and my dearest friend died of cancer. A couple long time friendships ended. My work seeing clients one-on-one felt false. I was preaching good word, but wasn't practicing my own wisdom.

Everything I have held precious in my life was seriously challenged, and coming undone all at once.

The most painful thing, was that I couldn't hear myself, or the God-of-my-heart. My inner voice was muddied with fear and self-doubt. I have survived a lot of external chaos with grace because I could hear and trust the still, small voice within me. The chaos was now inside of me, and everything was touched by it.

I needed freedom from the familiar to unwind myself and release the pain, so my husband and I packed up our car and began a year-long pilgrimage in search of home. We had a calling to the Pacific Northwest, and the closer we got, the more my inner voice began to come back. Once we landed, I experienced three invitations from within that pointed me in the direction of forgiveness, being seen and knowing that I am enough. From this generous new reality, self-love has had room to grow.

The Missing Piece in Self-Love

The first invitation: to forgive myself.

The sun's presence grew brighter and bigger in our bedroom, not so gently demanding my eyelids open. Before I could ritualistically put my feet on the floor to head towards the bathroom, a voice within asked me to stay with myself just a little longer. I have learned to abide this still, small voice.

In these raw and vulnerable moments upon waking, I was spontaneously viewing different scenarios from childhood onward where I lacked compassion for myself. I could see each moment from a bird's-eye-view. I witnessed how each choice to be unmerciful with myself affected others. I saw that I still carried all of these moments like a backpack filled with bricks.

The voice returned, and asked me if I was ready to forgive myself, and let my burden go.

I wasn't sure. Could I forgive myself? Was that a spiritual bypass, a cop-out?

Before I could think about it too much, my heart said "yes!"

A softness over-came me and I instantly felt lighter.

Forgiving myself removed the veils from my sight. Facing these moments that brought embarrassment, shame and pain, and letting it all go allowed me to see myself for what I really am: a woman who is worthy of forgiveness and love.

Forgiving myself was the first step to loving myself. Until that moment, a part of me believed that self-love was selfish. A lot of the messaging I received as a young person programmed me to think of others before myself. Most of my energy, identity, intelligence and effort has been directed towards serving others and the greater good. I was initiated into the healing arts as a very young person, and ordained through an inter-spiritual community a week after turning 30. All throughout my schooling I was appointed by my peers and faculty for peer support and counseling positions. Spiritual companionship and mediation are natural to me, and I've often been called upon to be of service.

I'm grateful for this.

Because of the path I have walked, I have cultivated an ability to truly listen. I've been blessed with moments of sheer delight by witnessing the healing and miracles of others.

Listening to myself and surrendering my burden opened me to the delight and miracle of my own healing. What a gift.

The second invitation: to allow myself to be seen.

The very next day, again before I was out of bed, another vision bubbled up. I saw myself as a 4 year old, angry and hurt because my mom was yelling at me about something I couldn't do anything about. I noticed how rooted I was in my body. My feet were planted firmly on the floor. I felt like a little brick house. My small self decided that I needed protection in that moment. I saw myself, and in fact remember, looking around the room to see what might make for a good shield. I never wanted to be caught off guard again. The thing that caught my eye was the soup pot on the stove. I imagined putting the stainless steel pot over me, and carving out a little hole for God. I already had a strong relationship with the God-of-my-heart, and was in tune enough to keep that line of communication open as a child.

This choice at 4 years old actually defined much of my adult life. This vision showed me how approaching my life from a position of protection impaired me. I saw that as much as I benefitted from having a shield and filter, I was also limited by it. I was always negotiating my safety in intimate relationships, and I rarely showed my true self. Tragic. It's hard enough to receive love without an imaginary steel wall blocking the way.

The still, small voice whispered to me that I didn't need protection, and maybe I could consider letting the wall fall away.

I let it down.

Light flooded my sight, and I saw myself standing naked on a beach. The sea air was whipping around me, cleansing me. My heart was a star, beaming brightly all around me.

Immediately after letting down my shield, everything in my present waking life began to open up. I was offered my dream job in a print shop, and other opportunities that made my heart sing. My light was visible to the world! My shadows are still present, and will always be, but they simply do not rule me.

Everything is different.

I see myself clearly: I am a woman with a light in her heart that is stronger than a shield of steel.

The third invitation was so simple and sweet, it could have been over-looked: I am enough.

I was at work, a place I love very much. My hands were busy and my heart was happy. I felt this wave vibrate my feet, moving upward in a warm rush throughout my entire body. My heart swelled, and I knew that I was enough.

I am beautiful enough. I am knowledgeable enough. I am enough.

I am spiritual enough.

I have enough.

I am enough.

The still, small voice was present and whispered to me, "You are enough as you are, enough as you are, enough as you are".

This "enoughness" hasn't left me.

It's easier to love myself, because I know I am enough.

My offering to you

What is presently highlighted for me in my practice of self-love, is that we do not need to have it all figured out. The journey of self-love is just that, a journey. We will never get to everything, fix everything, smooth every wrinkle, or lose every extra pound. There can be no end goal with self-love, for there is no end to who you are. We're enough as we are, and as we are becoming.

When we tend to ourselves with loving care, we open pathways to new experiences of ourselves. When we're as kind, tender, forgiving, and loving to ourselves as we are to others, we have what we need to give generously and honestly.

Some self-care is about taking action: eating well, movement, prayer and/or meditation, talking through blockages and celebrating successes, taking a hot bath, and let's get real here, getting occasional (or not so occasional) pedicures!

Some self-care is so quiet, so elusive, but no less potent and important: asking yourself what you need and following through, experiencing a moment of profound union, the gift of really receiving illuminating words from a stranger or a friend, minimizing how much crap you allow, forgiving yourself, letting your shield down.

Sometimes self-love is nourished unexpectedly by some Mysterious Something larger than you. Invitations are always being extended to you. Your delight will help you discern the invitations that are right for you.

The Missing Piece in Self-Love

Something that is notable about the invitations from my inner self and the God-of-my-heart, is that 2 out of 3 happened in the morning before I started my day. My invitation to you: upon waking, spend a few moments in solitude and stillness. Luxuriate in the fuzziness of being between dreaming and waking. Notice how you feel. If you're so inclined, ask yourself what would bring you delight. Ask yourself what might be blocking you from fully receiving your delight. Heed what you hear. Keep an open mind, open ears, open eyes throughout your day. You may receive impulses, messages, synchronicities, gut feelings that nourish your connection with yourself.

This life is precious.

You are enough.

Compiled By Kate Gardner

Mofoluwaso Ilevbare

Mofoluwaso Ilevbare (Fofo) is a Vibrant Life & Leadership Coach, Speaker & Trainer.

Her life oozes energy, passion and a desire to see every little girl, teen, and woman soar, free to fly above all cultural, social, physical & emotional limits and live her fullest potential.

Having overcome underlying beliefs, life challenges and two near-death experiences, Fofo's heart beats for "living every day with no regrets". Her legacy will be "Fear Less. Press Forward. Live Your Purpose".

A social entrepreneur & women-empowering advocate, Fofo champions a charity, (www.wcbpurpose.org), inspiring women and young girls in Africa and around the world. She loves God, loves life, and loves to bring out the best in others.

You can reach Fofo at:

E-mail:
fofoilev@gmail.com

LinkedIn:
https://www.linkedin.com/in/mofoluwasoilevbare

Blog:
http://www.lifecoachingwithfofo.com/

Website:
http://www.johncmaxwellgroup.com/mofoluwasoilevbare

Facebook:
https://www.facebook.com/fofoilev

Compiled By Kate Gardner

Beauty and the Beast

By Mofoluwaso Ilevbare

It was a different kind of night. The clouds were unusually darker. Looking at the sky, there were no stars in sight. In the distance, the neighborhood cock crowed viciously, as if it knew that something historic was about to happen.

On top of the Orotan hill stood the king's palace, surrounded by a beautiful garden filled with purple tulips and orange trees. A cry in the distance signaled that something was going on. Listening closely, it sounded like a woman in pain, her voice ringing with anguish, the tone wreaked with fear.

The voice belonged to Omolabake, the third wife of the King of Orotan. Indeed, she was in pain but not just any type of pain. Nine months had passed by so quickly, and it was time for her to be strong and push out the baby in her womb. The royal midwives gathered round, doing their best to assist her on this journey every pregnant woman must take alone. On the balcony, at the left hand side of the palace, the King waited in his chamber, pacing up and down, eagerly waiting for the joyous news. "Could this baby be the crown prince of Orotan Kingdom?" he thought to himself. The pastors of the land had predicted, the wishes of the people had gone forth. This was the reason he had married a third wife- not because he did not adore the nine princesses he already had from two wives, he desperately needed an heir, a crowned prince to carry on the lineage.

And so they waited, as Omolabake pushed with all the strength she had inside. The labour went on for at least three hours. Then suddenly, a different cry, a fresh voice was heard, and hope sprang up in the hearts of all who were near. The baby was here. As the midwife cut off the umbilical cord and wrapped the child, silence filled the room. The emissary hurried to alert the King in his palace and deliver the news of the birth of his child. Everyone present wanted to know if the crown prince was finally born. As the King walked out to meet the people, his countenance said it all. It should have been a boy.

THE LONG AWAITED ONE

In my culture, having a male child is seen as very significant and important in any family lineage. It is not uncommon to find couples trying again and again, or praying and trusting God for a male child.

My birth was surrounded by a similar anticipation, the fourth in the family after 3 girls. Many positive declarations had been made, the optimism was high. There were no sophisticated 3D ultrasound scanners back then when my mother was pregnant. People depended mostly on prophesies, signs, and sometimes the use of traditional herbs to know/predict the sex of a child. In my case, I was to be the long awaited one.

Alas, a bouncing baby girl was born, innocent looking, oblivious of the circumstances in which she came, surrounded my mixed feelings of joy and disappointment.

As I grew older, it became clearer to me. Hearing those words "you should have been a boy" often left me feeling a bit unwanted. Sometimes, I would ask myself "Why am I here?" To make matters worse, I loved playing soccer barefoot in the streets, climbing trees with thorns, typical things we've been stereotyped to believe only boys do.

As I grew into a teenager, the contrasts increased. While many of my friends looked elegant and tall, I was short and plump, with chubby legs. They seemed lady-like, I was labelled "tomboyish". For a while, I even wore only ankle-length skirts to hide my legs.

My quest to find my purpose and my place in the world continued until one day, it hit me. The more I discovered the unique talents that I had, the more excited I became. As my faith in God grew, so did my awareness about who I was, that I was fearfully and wonderfully made, and that He loved me no matter what. I began to love me for me.

I was special. I was loved. I was unique. And most of all, I was meant to be here.

In as much as my parents and sisters loved me, embracing God's love and loving myself was the ultimate. I learnt to forgive anyone who had hurt me along the way, and I developed a passion to help others who felt the same way. I stopped comparing myself to others, and instead dug deeper within myself and let ME shine.

Fast forward to fifteen years later. I sat and watched as my pre-schooler read his bed time story book aloud. It was the classic story of "The Beauty and the Beast". As he flipped through the pages, my mind wandered away. I could picture in my mind the pretty princess, curly brown hair neatly packed with pink ribbons, blue eyes, a pretty smile and pointed toes. Then the picture flipped to a darker side, and I could see the beast. Not sure if I could refer to the creature as "he" or "it". His big sunken eyes looked right at me and I felt my heart shudder. His hands reminded me of wolverine in the X-men movies, only I could not see the metal prongs shooting out from his fingers. Big, bushy black hair, and a voice that sounded like ..... "Mum, are you listening?" I suddenly heard my son say..and it brought me back

The Missing Piece in Self-Love

to reality. Phew! "Where were we?" I said and chuckled as I laughed at myself and my imagination.

Weeks later, as I prepared for my next speaking engagement, thoughts about the Beauty and the Beast came flushing back to my mind. Could the beauty and the beast really co-habit?

The irony of life is that behind every beauty lurks a beast. Behind every good thing lurks a dark side. The constant tug of war between good and evil, like and dislike, healthy and unhealthy, smooth and rough, is an integral part of our lives. It's like the nagging voice in your head, only you can hear, telling you "You're not good enough. You're not strong enough. You're not worthy to be seen. You don't deserve a good life".

Do you want to know the missing piece in self-love?

Here is my answer.

You've got to love yourself the way God loves you, see yourself the way God sees you, take care of yourself the way God does, embrace yourself the way He embraces you- perfectly created, divinely crafted, unique and chosen for such a time as this.

Every day when you wake up, you can choose to see the beauty of a new day or the beast of a million issues wrong in the world.

Every day when you set out, you can choose to unleash the beautiful you that God made or choose to see the beast: the parts of your body you don't like, the fact that you're fat, skinny, dimpled, or freckled, the fact that you stammer, are an introvert, or otherwise.

Every day, you can choose to unleash the beauty in your voice and follow your dreams or be intimidated by the beast and choose to be passive.

Compiled By Kate Gardner

THE FIGHT WITHIN

In our minds is a constant tug of war between the beauty and the beast. Many at times, it is not about what others have to say about you, rather it is the about the conflicting connection within your spirit, your soul and your body to embrace yourself for who you truly are inside, no masks, no make-up, just you.

Imagine an actor/actress expected to open the grand scene of a movie, walking in on stage with less than himself/herself. The enthusiasm of the crowd disappears and the movie may never become a hit.

In the same way, life is like a big stage and we are all actors in it.

If you want to be anything, get up with a sense of purpose and go be that thing! Enough of following people who undermine your strengths. Enough of listening to those who will only deflate your dreams. You've got one life to live, make it fabulous! Take your place and play your part as best as you can because, once the curtains are drawn, there's not much you can do anymore.

Who dictates whether as a girl has to play football or dollhouse?

Who says men don't cry?

I am grateful for my journey to self-love and as I share this with you, I hope it encourages you to open the doors of your heart to embrace who you truly are. You are special! You can make a difference! You are beautiful and you MATTER!

Reflection:

Today, take a good look at yourself in the mirror, pause for a moment and really take a good look at yourself. Can you see the beauty not the beast?

The Missing Piece in Self-Love

Nathaniel J. Grisgsby

Nathaniel J. Grigsby was born in September 1987, in Southern California. His life was that of a top competitor in Alpine ski racing, holding gold from Junior Olympics, and the top 5 placings in a few international races. His struggles with drugs and alcohol led him to prison, along with the lifestyle of running with a street gang for many years. Fortunately, he found himself getting sober and, ultimately, helping others in recovery, especially with the gift of the body art he gives each client through his tattoo work. Today his drive and ambition is helping others to find their way to loving themselves again, through words or art, one piece at a time

You can reach Nathaniel at:

Email:
nathanielgrigsby6@gmail.com

Website:
www.inktherapylansing.com

Facebook:
Nate Grigsby

Compiled By Kate Gardner

From Slopes to Syringes to Serenity
By Nathaniel J. Grigsby

From the time I turned eight years old, my mother and uncle exposed me to what became a life passion of mine when they took me on my first experience on the slopes of Mountain High Resort in Wrightwood, California. From then on I was a natural born skier. By the next ski season, while I was still only eight years old, I entered into the world of ski racing.

After years of hard work, competitions, struggles, I won my first junior Olympics at Mt. Hood, Oregon, winning 3 gold medals by the age of fourteen. It was at that race I suffered a freak accident that caused me to no longer be able to compete. A gate smashed my knee cap while racing. Even though I had an operation and extensive rehab, my knee was never the same. I was no longer the skier I was before, but I pushed on. Because of my accomplishments I was noticed by all of my sponsors, and was introduced to the next level of competition.

I was ranked #1 over-all in the Nation in my age division, earned a spot on the US Development Race Team, and was a top FIS race competitor. My racing career took off, and I found myself in countries all over the world; Argentina, Switzerland, Norway and Canada. It's during that same time in my racing career that I became a heavy drinker.

I was kicked off my Team while at a FIS race at Big Sky, Montana, and that is where my racing career ended. My life was no longer the same, and I soon turned to drugs and alcohol on a daily basis. Not long afterwards, I was kicked out of my high school and had to enter into continuation school so I could graduate. I still got to walk with my graduating class. After graduation, my Mom began to notice my drug use and stepped in. She encouraged me to move to Portland, Oregon to attend Culinary school with my older brother.

Hoping a geographical change would be the answer to my addiction, I learned quickly that a change of scenery wasn't the way to solve my problems. The move to Oregon put me on the path of drug dealing, robbery, and all that pertains to the criminal lifestyle. That is when I left Oregon, leaving school behind. I made it back to San Diego, California where I got into psychedelics and met a group of guys that made me feel as if I was part of a family. This is when the real criminal empire was exposed to me, and the gang banging started.

I was placed on my first out of state drug movement mission. Some of the states I was sent to included Kansas, Missouri, Colorado, and Arizona. Trafficking, distributing, and laundering are some of the few high risk tasks this 'job' included.

Soon enough the heat was on from the police, and I was under watch for my activity. It was time to get back to California. A few months of being back home, I caught my first charge that led me to my first prison term. After getting to prison, I reconnected with my family, and I found a new mission; the California prison politics and in-state drug trafficking and distribution, mainly working with the Mexican Mafia.

For the next nine and a half years, I had accumulated two more prison terms from stealing fire arms to assault charges. I was in and out of prison with an extremely high amount of drug use and gang related activities that one wouldn't even fathom.

It wasn't until my last prison term when reality finally hit me. I was recognizing all the wrong I had done and wanted out of the prison life style. I finally reached out to Shelly Mangold, my drug and alcohol counselor in prison. I asked if I could be paroled into a residential treatment program. One month later I was released to Inland Valley Recovery Services in Upland, CA. My sole purpose and focus was on not returning to prison.

Within six months I became 'Head of House', and was enrolled into college for graphic design. I was being recognized for the progress I was making. I would like to say that my life stayed in positive progress in my recovery, but just as things were starting to come together for me, and I thought I had things under control, I found myself leaving the program to run back to my comfort zone, my wife, the needle.

Ironically, the motel I went to that night was right across the street from the same hotel that the stabbing incident had occurred which had sent me to my last prison term. While being at the motel on a couple of days binge, I was working with a woman named Esther Gibson, to get myself into a sober living house which my parole would pay for, for nine months. After arriving there I got a job fairly quickly as a dog groomer, and was attending college again.

After six months of doing really well, I got a new roommate. Within twenty four hours, he and I were both using drugs. Within a matter of weeks he was kicked out, and I had thrown away my school yet again. I also ended up leaving and, before I knew it, I was back to running the streets with the homies.

It wasn't long before I lost my job, and was giving false addresses to my parole agent, instead of the information agreed upon in my parole guidelines. While running the streets, I had gone back to the criminal behavior I was so sure I was ready to let go of a year ago. Between selling used cars and tattooing, I finally had enough proof of income for my parole agent. But, my main source of income was the large amounts of methamphetamine I was pushing in California. The day finally came when my parole agent called me with the news I would be discharged from parole. I was a free man, yet I still hadn't had enough.

Between the deaths of my best friend, a close friend's daughter, a driver of mine and my neighbour, who overdosed on pills bought from us, it was enough to keep me using. After those deaths, my Mom suggested that I leave California and go to Florida to meet my biological father. The next day I boarded a Greyhound bus to Live Oak, FL. Without my parent's knowledge, I had brought a quarter ounce of meth with me that lasted me two weeks, which would make my last use on December, 16th 2014.

I'd be lying if I said that this was my last use by choice. I didn't want to quit using, I wasn't ready. Little did I know, my road to recovery was soon to be in my path after six months of hard struggle to survive in Florida. After talking with my mom and making one phone call to a place called RISE that my mom's best friend referred me to, it was time to take a step out of my comfort zone and go in a direction to an unknown destination for success. The day after the phone call was made, I was ready, packed my things and boarded a plane to Lansing, Michigan.

Upon arrival to RISE, I learned that I had yet again gotten myself into a transitional sober living house. I enrolled into college right away, and was hired at a tattoo shop that is affiliated with RISE. I have been pursuing my work as a tattoo artist at the tattoo shop that the owners of Rise own called INK THERAPY LANSING

After a few weeks of being a part of RISE, and truly working my program, reuniting with old friends and family members, I was encouraged to put my story on paper to share my experiences, struggles, strengths and new outlooks on life, to relay the message in recovery and help other struggling addicts.

No matter what you have gone through, or are going through, giving up is not the answer! Taking steps you are unsure of **can** lead to positive outcomes. Accepting life on life's terms, having a full understanding of the laws of attraction, taking action on all of the goals I've set for myself - regardless of how many obstacles I'm put through in the process, I keep moving forward by any means necessary. No longer taking assignments and missions from others, I am making my own hopes and dreams, and creating my own destiny.

With a positive attitude, determination, and hard work anything can be achieved without having to resort to drugs or drinking. Not being afraid to ask for direction, taking advice, and taking the steps that seem uncomfortable. Remaining positive, humbling myself, and starting from the bottom while having an open mind, is opening the doors to the universe's blessings in my life.

The Missing Piece in Self-Love

Pam Robertson

Dr. Pam Robertson works as a coach, consultant, and professional speaker. Pam is regularly sought out for advice by the career and life flummoxed and she has worked with people from A-Z, literally accountants to zoo-keepers and many occupations in between.

Pam has been published in several best sellers, and is a life-long consumer of education. She has completed a degree in education, a master's degree, and a doctorate in interdisciplinary studies, focussing on career development. Pam has been certified as a coach, an HR practitioner, a professional writer, and at one time completed several levels of musicianship. These days she is messing up the kitchen in her spare time, and posting food pics all over social media.

You can reach Pam at:

Website:
http://www.ladybirdfiles.com

Facebook:
https://www.Facebook.com/BeBoldBeBraveBeBrilliant

Compiled By Kate Gardner

Twitter:
https://www.twitter.com/PamRobertson

Instagram:
PamDRobertson

The Missing Piece in Self-Love

Digging In

By Pam Robertson

When I first stepped up to write for this book, I figured writing my chapter was going to be pretty easy. It would be a vehicle for me to share something that people need to know, obviously, and if my little piece could help just one person live a bigger, bolder life, then that would be brilliant.

So I wrote my chapter, and it was a decent story all about looking after myself and how I fought my way back from different crappy events in my life to get things to where I appreciated them. And then I sat on that story for three weeks, dreading that anyone would read it. The trouble with that chapter was that it was more about putting on a good face and giving a reader a good read. It wasn't about the real ugly thing I am dealing with when it comes to appreciating me.

So I sat down and started to re-think things and put them in order. I created an outline about what's really important to me that could help someone who reads this chapter in a much bigger way. Instead, I offer you the story of how I came to accept that one final unlikable piece of myself, by digging in. Don't get me wrong – I see myself as a happy, well-adjusted individual. I know what it takes to look after me, I am good at it, and I like my own company. However, the not so very big secret has been this up and down relationship I have with food.

While some people have a love-hate relationship with food, mine has always been a love-love relationship. I enjoy eating. I love to cook. I use food like a drinker uses alcohol (and I like to cook with liquor too). Sure, I use food for sustenance, but I've also used it to soothe myself after a tough day, and I can eat when I am bored, or eat to stay awake and meet deadlines, and I eat for the sake of eating. I'm one of those people that can find every drive thru in town, even when I am visiting a place for the first time.

I hope it's okay with you that I am still a work in progress on this front. I'm still managing this part of my life every single day, but it's getting easier.

I don't have a naturally slim physique, something which was made painfully true to me in school gym classes, and reinforced throughout adulthood, and even while in the army I was at least slightly overweight. I am one of those people that had a ten pound baby and came out of the hospital after delivering my son having lost exactly ten pounds, and not another pound left my body for months.

Food and I have a great history. I'm pretty sure I was a foodie before someone even invented the word. When I was at university they had these giant cinnamon buns with big sugar crystals on the top. Who the heck wants to buy a plate of salad for $6 when a cinnamon bun was only $2.50 and was so darned satisfying?

When my family hosted a seasonal or holiday gathering, the table would groan under the weight of platters of rich delights like scotch eggs, potato salad, meat dishes, pastas, all served alongside freshly turned out buns or garlic bread. Then the table would get cleared off for the dessert round where the savouries were replaced by multiple cakes, pastries, and chocolate. And the sweeter and richer the food was, the happier my food brain was.

I bought into the concept that I needed to increase my exercise so that calories going out exceeded calories going in. I tried all kinds of exercise, and when I asked an exercise therapist about my lacklustre results, he said that I just hadn't found "my *thing*" yet. Once I found an activity I really loved, he promised, I'd get fit and never worry about my weight again.

One night I balled up plenty of courage and went to a presentation about obesity. The doctor made it clear that while there is all kinds of information on nutrition and exercise, the biggest problem is that the highest weight you ever achieve becomes a **set point** for weight that is very comfortably accepted by our brain. Desire, exercise, and diet alone cannot change this set point. I left the presentation thinking that if I was struggling against a set point my issue was not about finding exercise I enjoyed, or about eating an additional pound of leafy greens every day. Although diet and exercise are important, my being overweight was a thought strategy. A head game if you will. Finally, I had found my *thing*!

Not long after hearing that doctor speak came a day where I went to visit my doctor. He said that my blood levels would be fine if I were an 80 year old but, being 49 meant they were unacceptable. Jeez, that hurt, but I knew I had been failing with that head game of mine, so I figured I had better dig in and make something happen. The set point issue was weighing heavily on my mind.

Firstly, I arranged for some heartfelt conversations with a nutritionist and a dietician. They gave me some great recipes, the occasional, "you can do this!" and a "go for it" kind of mantra. They had not heard of the set point idea, and couldn't help with it.

I needed a different approach.

Instead of fighting food and feeling frustrated about the state of my health, I had to face the fact that my physical body was up to me. I was going to have to find a way to deliberately change my results, and my body, and I knew that meant I needed an attitude adjustment.

I mentioned this is a work in progress right? Because I have to tell you, dammit, this is hard work.

I pulled out some of the material I use in coaching and reviewed everything I could on mindset (most of which was related to how we think about money, but I figured the approach was probably going to be the same). I reviewed the things I had taught others about the terror barrier and how to create a breakthrough that would last. And I enlisted the help of my family.

To kick things off, I spent four weeks with my mum. She was up for the company because my dad was away travelling, and so their kitchen became an experimental zone. I grabbed recipes from Pinterest and we played with some really simple, very tasty dishes. Then we added things like chutney or a simple dressing that made them even better. Then we tried them all again and did some tweaking to adjust them to our tastes. In that four weeks, I peeled. I diced. I marinated. I minced. I barbecued. I steamed.

I deliberately considered how these decisions about food were instrumental in breaking free and embracing a healthier life.

Another big shift was that I looked at my plate before digging in, and appreciated what was there and how it was working for me instead of just being mindlessly eaten. I worked on being grateful. And that's when I dug a little deeper and acknowledged that part of my shift was to stop thinking that only certain types of food really made me feel satisfied.

After the four weeks with Mum, I was happy to see my blood pressure and blood tests were in the normal range some of the time. This was not a usual occurrence for me and we celebrated by planting more seeds in the garden.

The Missing Piece in Self-Love

I falter now and then, but I keep putting myself back on the path. My daughter is helping by keeping the fridge filled with farmer's market finds, and chopped veggies that we can go to instead of heading toward the junk aisle at the store. Instead of making jams this summer, I am focussing on chutneys as a way to embellish a dish, and I feel really good about it.

I am still a work in progress on the set point issue. I'm still enamoured with food, but it's about making choices. I'm still managing this thing every single day, but I'm loving where I've come so far. I know I can do this because I *get* what it means to establish a new set point, and I get what it means to do this work. It's about reprogramming my subconscious with a new set point, and getting results helps me live my motto, **Live Inspired**.

I *love* the foodie in me. I love food. I appreciate that now I can look at food differently than I ever have, and that when I dig in to enjoy a meal it's about honouring who I am and where I've come. To me, that's the epitome of self-love on the food scale.

Now, let's dig in!

Compiled By Kate Gardner

Patricia LeBlanc, RMT, IARP

Patricia LeBlanc inspires and motivates others to manifest their goals and dreams. Patricia is passionate about helping others to live a happy and abundant life. Using a holistic approach, she helps her clients to get out of their own way and she teaches them how to manifest their goals, dreams, and desires into their life.

Patricia is an Award Winning Author, Speaker, Certified Attraction Abundance Coach, Master Energy Practitioner/ Teacher. She is the compiler of the upcoming Anthology Book called Manifesting a New Life: Money, Love, Health and everything in between being released in Sept 2015.

You can contact Patricia at:

Phone:
1-647-977-6987

Email:
info@patricialeblanc.ca

Website:
www.patriciaeleblanc.com
www.manifestinganewlife.com

Facebook:
www.facebook.com/leblancpatricia1

LinkedIn:
https://ca.linkedin.com/in/leblancpatricia

Twitter:
www.twitter.com/leblancpatricia

Compiled By Kate Gardner

My Journey from Hating to Accepting and Loving Myself
By Patricia LeBlanc, RMT, IARP

Several years ago, if you told me that I would now be able to say with confidence and in loving energy that I love and accept myself for who I truly am, I would have laughed in your face. I would have been on the floor laughing, literally. I would have told you that you were crazy.

For years I used to deeply HATE myself, as I did not feel worthy of being loved. This goes way back to my childhood. As a child I was bullied and did not feel accepted. I also did not fit in with most of my family or society in general. It did not help that I was an empath, and did not know how to protect myself from toxic people. I did not know how to set boundaries with others, especially with narcissism. I would take any abuse that was thrown to me.

As you can imagine, all of this affected my self-confidence and affected me in ways that would stay with me for years. I did not feel worthy of being loved, so how could I love myself? How could I be in a healthy relationship with anyone including myself? I got myself in several toxic relationships. One of those relationship got so bad that I actually feared for my life. The day that I left him, I pressed charges and now he has a criminal record. I was prone to minor depressions, in part due to genetics, and in part due to the fact that I did not love myself. At times, I wanted to kill myself, as I did not feel loved or worthy of living.

The Missing Piece in Self-Love

In 2004, I was diagnosed with major depression. I hit rock bottom. I did not want to do anything. I took me several months to start coming back up. It was my wake-up call. I knew I needed to make major changes and I needed to start loving myself. I did a 360 degree life evaluation. Who was I? What did I want? What did I love about myself? What did others love about me? Why was I put on the Earth? What was my mission? What flaws did I have, and how could I learn to accept them without feeling I needed to be perfect?

It took me about 5 years to start really loving myself, and in the last year I finally fell in love with myself. I now completely and fully accept and love myself. I am now ready to be in a healthy and loving relationship with my male soul mate.

It took me over 10 years to discover who I truly was, and what my life purpose is. Was it an easy journey? Hell no! But, the journey has been worth it. I know now that I needed to go thru this in order to help others to be able to love themselves and manifest the life that they truly wanted. These experiences have also allowed me to help other people heal themselves, while discovering who they are and what they want in life.

In this process, I have met the most amazing people. I have made friends with so many incredible people. I am blessed to now be able to say that I love myself and my life. I have the most loving friends, and attract only love into my life. I manifest the most amazing things with ease and grace. I am able to attract all of this because I am now coming from the energy of love. Now do I always come from an energy of love, no, I do not, as I am human and fall back down. I sometimes will beat myself up, but it now doesn't last long as I choose to be love and to love myself. Make the decision today, right now, that you will love yourself no matter what. The magic will start as what you think about, your body follow. I LOVE MYSELF FULLY AND COMPLETELY.

How I learned to Love myself?

I am going to provide you with my tips on how I came to love myself. You can take what works for you and use it. You can discard what doesn't work or resonate with you. This is a good starting point for you to start loving yourself.

1. Spend time alone. It is very important to spend some 'me' time. IN order to stay aligned with yourself, you need to spend some alone time. It is not easy to do, but you need to schedule that 'me' time every single day. It's also very important to spend time alone in order to love yourself. If you are not comfortable spending time alone with yourself, you have a major problem.
2. Pamper yourself. It is very important to do something for you that you love every single day. It can be buying flowers for yourself, going to the spa, getting a massage or manicure/pedicure. It could be spending time in nature, reading, doing yoga. It could be taking a nice bubble bath with candles. Pamper yourself.
3. Energy Healing Session. Energy Healing has allowed me to release a lot of my toxic experiences and past. It has also allowed me to rediscover who I am. I am so grateful for discovering Reiki in 2007 and becoming a Reiki Master in 2008. I am also blessed that I discovered IET in 2008 and became an IET Master Instructor in 2013. The impact of Having Reiki and IET in my life, is simply magical. Not only have I seen the results on myself, I have witnessed the magical changes in my clients. If this resonates with you, then please feel free to contact me to for a free consultation, to see if this can help you.

The Missing Piece in Self-Love

4. Release your past. Let go of your past and forgive yourself for all the mistakes you made. You are not perfect and should stop beating yourself up because you made a mistake. A lot of time, we can forgive others but cannot forgive ourselves. Release it and forgive yourself.
5. Discover who you are. It is very important to discover who you truly are. In order to accept yourself and love YOU. If you do not know who you are then I highly recommend that you start making the time to do so. Discover what you love and what you don't. Discover what you are good at and what you are not so good at. You need to spend time reflecting these questions. You can meditate on these questions. I would start a journal for this very specific purpose and make it unique and fill it with love.
6. Accept yourself. In order to truly love yourself, you need to accept the good and the bad. You are perfect the way that you are. True love happens when you accept and love yourself fully. This means that when you can accept your qualities as well as your faults, only then can you truly love yourself. Remember no one is perfect, and neither are you. You are unique and should embrace that.
7. Affirmations: Start by using powerful affirmations. I am is the most powerful words that you can ever tell yourself. Start by creating your affirmation. Here are some examples to help you out. I am Love. I am worthy of Love. I Love Myself. Once you have finished writing your affirmation, start by writing them on a nice piece of colorful paper and then record them. Listen to them and read them several times a day. What comes to your mind when you say or read them? If you hear a little voice telling you no you're not… Send it some love. I send it love by saying thank you for your opinion, but I am not taking it on and repeat my affirmation several times. You see when you come from a place of love,

you will attract more love into your life. If you get upset at it, then guess what, you will attract more negativity into your life. Now you see why it is important to be love and come from an energy of love.

Conclusion

My hope is for you to learn to accept yourself for your qualities as well as your faults. Remember, if you want to be in a healthy loving relationship, then it all starts within. Love yourself, because you are worthy of being loved. Love yourself, because you are LOVE. Radiate that love and watch magic happen around you. You have one life, so you might as well live a loving life. Watch what loving things/people/opportunities you will attract into your life when you come from an energy of love.

Lots of LOVE, Patricia LeBlanc xoxo

Richelle Traversano

Richelle Traversano is an international best-selling author and writer and is a motorcycle and life enthusiast. Her various non-fiction book collaborations are excellent examples that, with tenacity and a change of perspective, you can overcome and conquer obstacles in your life. Richelle is embarking on a journey of fiction writing and poetry series this year, and is a firm believer in copious amounts of laughter, good books and chocolate. She is learning to navigate through the world since the loss of her Mother, and will hug you tighter and longer than sometimes necessary. Richelle is a proud Canadian but prefers American pricing.

You can contact Richelle at:

Blog:
www.richellewrites.com

Email:
richelleauthoress@gmail.com

Facebook:
www.facebook.com/richelle.traversano

Compiled By Kate Gardner

Instagram:
www.instagram.com/richellechucklesgiggles

Twitter:
@chucklesgiggles

The Missing Piece in Self-Love

Ear of the Beholder
By Richelle Traversano

I have been in love with words my entire life. From an early age, I loved to speak them, write them, read them, and sing them. Many things occupied my youth including an abundance of books and music. Every book I read and each song I heard made me fall deeper in love with language and melodies. I am entirely smitten by the power of words.

At the age of nine, I was given a typewriter as a gift from my parents. That present was the equivalent of gifting me a candy store or a treasure chest or my very own island complete with every toy and good thing imaginable on it. My imagination was brought to life with each key stroke. Creating new worlds and epic adventures on paper was the beginning of my love affair with writing, one that I court to this day.

As much as I enjoyed writing, I also loved to sing. It was not uncommon to find me in my room with my hair brush in hand being used as a makeshift microphone, belting out tunes as I sang along with the radio, record player or ghetto blaster. I didn't have a favourite genre because I loved them all (and still do). If writing was likened to my favourite sundae and covered with oozing sweet caramel and chocolate sauces, then music was the extra scoop of ice-cream with a delicious cherry on top.

As childhood requires, I subjected my little sister to numerous one woman concerts starring myself. Whether she liked it or not, she was my fandom!

When it was nice weather outside, I moved the concerts outdoors.

Compiled By Kate Gardner

Our house was right beside a large park that consisted of a baseball diamond, a hockey rink, and an assortment of playground equipment as well as a large green area that was used for all sorts of childhood shenanigans. It was essentially an outdoor concert venue in my eyes. I could sing from the bleachers, or I could hum a tune from the swings. On the occasions where I couldn't maintain my sister's co-operation to be my audience, I could be found reading on the monkey bars. That park was an oasis of possibilities the same way my typewriter held the key to unwritten adventures waiting to be brought to life.

In junior high school, as a young teenager, I realized that my singing ability required instruction and refinement. I wanted to learn how to sing and to emote the way the smooth and soulful voices that filled my room, my head and my heart did when I played records and tapes - or even my Dad's old 8-track cassettes.

I knew that the more a person wrote, the better they would become at it. It's a skill you acquire by practice, one that can be learned. So I applied this logic to singing. Perhaps if I practiced often, one day I might be able to sing like those beautiful voices that spoke to my soul and touched it deeply - that's what I hoped for.

I would need a hand with this endeavour. I would need a singing teacher. And as luck would have it, or just simple happenstance, I came across an advertisement for singing lessons pinned to the bulletin board at the library I frequented. I copied down the phone number and ran home. I discussed the lessons with my parents, got the green light from them to sign up, and then I made the phone call.

The singing teacher lived just a short bike ride away from my house. I rode to my first lesson full of eager hope and anticipation. I was going to learn how to sing!

The Missing Piece in Self-Love

My singing teacher always sat at her piano with a tight smile and stern look on her face. Habitually, she had a glass of water placed on the edge of the top of the piano. Each lesson, she would lead me through the warm up, the scales and then a song. Forty-five minutes later she would take a sip from her water and that was my cue that the lesson was finished. Five weeks in, she asked me if my intention was to be singer. I told her not as a profession. I wanted to learn the skill because I loved to learn about anything I had a passion for. Her reply was 'good'. I understand what that comment meant now, however, at the time, I took that word for face value.

Six lessons came and went. During my seventh, she asked me what my favourite song was to sing. I told her, she then proceeded to run me through the notes and instructed me to practice it every day. And I did. I sang it incessantly, much to my family's chagrin.

The eighth lesson was more than just a singing lesson. It was a life lesson.

She told me to sit down. Strange, as this was not the usual procedure. We sat in silence for what felt like hours. I finally asked if she would like to hear the song I practiced. My question was ignored. Just before I was about to ask another one, she picked up the glass of water that adorned the top of her piano and clutched it between both hands. I was confused by her actions and non-actions as well. She broke the silence after what felt like even more hours passing by and told me to sing the song. I managed to expel the first verse only, before she signaled me to stop. She sipped from the glass and her face went flush. At this point I was entirely confused.

"Do you know what's in this glass?" she asked. "Water?" I replied with even more confusion. "No, today this is not water. For twenty years it's been water but not today. Today it's Vodka."

I was only thirteen; I had no response to that.

She proceeded to explain that for her entire teaching career, I was the first student she couldn't teach. She had students that went on to sing for the opera and even one who became part of a popular touring band but, at the very least, all the students could carry a tune. Not me. I asked why she waited eight lessons to educate me on my ear piercing voice. She said she was waiting for a miracle.

Ouch.

Her words were like thieves in the night. They robbed me. And at the tender age of thirteen, her words had enough power to alter my confidence. I felt less than. I had affected her so negatively that she chose to drink alcohol to cope. I could handle the reality that I was not meant to sing. However, expecting me to shoulder the blame for her drinking was unacceptable. But that's exactly what I did for the longest time. That is a heavy weight for anyone to carry. It took a long time to understand that I was not responsible for that or for her. She was.

That experience, and every lesson born from it, taught me first and foremost to love myself enough to not accept the blame for anyone's shortcomings and to never blame anyone for mine.

Adults get it wrong sometimes. And, as an adult, I can testify to that truth. I forgave that teacher a long, long time ago, for my own well-being. That day ignited something deep down inside of me and I use that spark to this very day. When rejections or hard truths are at hand, I do not let the words penetrate like a deep wound. Instead, I take what I can from the experience and move on with a little more knowledge about life. As well as a little more self-love and a missing piece to the puzzle about people, places and or things. I learned that a person does not need a 'thick skin' mentality, as we're so often told. But we can choose our perspectives - and that can determine how a person journeys through their individual circumstance and experience.

I have loved words my entire life, with all of their glorious uses and anatomy. I may not be able to articulate them gracefully through song, but that will never stop me from participating, or enjoying anything that I love to do. Not being able to sing like the majestic voices that vibrate through this universe is not the end of the world for me. I have an acute appreciation for writers, singers, painters, artists, photographers, and all creators in their various forms, trades and outlets. I am in constant awe of a melodic voice or beautifully written words.

We may not be grand at all things, but we can be great at a lot of things.

My apologies are offered through this book to my neighbours, passers-by on the street, and to all Karaoke attendants and fellow concert goers for the days that my inner super star dismisses that teacher's words and just sings anyway.

Compiled By Kate Gardner

Shannon Hrobak Sennefelder

Shannon Hrobak Sennefelder, Resilience Expert, Author, Certified Performance Coach and Certified Relationship Coach serves as the President of White Swans Consulting, LLC. Shannon is an Amazon International Best Selling Author and nationally recognized speaker. Shannon is a champion for creating powerful experiences that leave a lasting connection with clients. She creates an environment where individuals can examine personal choices proactively. She and her team establish structures necessary to achieve an understanding of key barriers and the realization of the desired outcomes.

You can contact Shannon at:

Phone:
570.952.4650

Website:
www.whiteswansconsulting.com

The Missing Piece in Self-Love

Look Around You
By Shannon Hrobak Sennefelder

Over twenty years ago, I was involved in an abusive relationship. The physical violence wore on me, but not as much as the emotional pain. Years of being told that I'm not good enough or smart enough became my truth. I felt worthless and lost my will to live. Yet with the help of relentless friends and my own faith, I found the strength to stand up again. Eventually, I found my voice and was able to escape the violence.

Many people ask me: "How did you overcome your shame?" For me, it was one moment that changed the course of who I was and how I would live my life. Remember my abuser? He was also the father of my twin daughters. One day, while preparing a bottle for my daughter, he broke in, drunk, like countless times before. He was visibly angry and wanted me to give him my daughter who was nestled in my arms. I said, "No way. You're drunk. You can't hold her when you're like this." He came towards me, enraged and in an instant kicked me in my stomach. I fell back onto the floor, my daughter thumping onto my chest.

That moment changed me. I decided right then, "No one will ever come between my daughters and me. I will never allow anyone to control me again." I found my voice. And I trust that you will find yours.

I know now that I found the strength to speak up because I no longer felt alone. I risked judgement and shared the truth about what was really happening in my relationship. Sure, I was embarrassed and ashamed. Mostly, I felt relief. I no longer kept my pain secret. Like so many people before me, I chose to take a stand for myself.

Every day we are faced with both darkness and light: in our choices, our relationships and especially in our internal dialogue. I have spent the majority of my adult life struggling with my own and others' darkness. Yet for some reason, I've always been able to find the light.

I *am* resilient, and so are you. I believe that as long as we are breathing, we have the opportunity to make changes in our lives. We each have the innate ability to stand up, speak up and overcome any of life's challenges. For many, this sounds like pie-in-the-sky nonsense. For me, and the countless women and men that I have worked with, it is truly living. For all of us, it is RESILIENCE.

Resiliency is defined by Webster's Dictionary as "the ability to overcome challenges of all kinds–trauma, tragedy, personal crises, and bounce back stronger, wiser, and more personally powerful. "

Cultivating resilience means operating at a deep structural, systemic, human level. It takes time and effort. Now brace yourself, it also takes patience to reach the point where you begin to feel resilient. Throughout the years, I've identified two steps that those before you have taken:

Step One. Find Someone Resilient To Connect With

What's essential is finding people who have a clear connection to their own resilience. The cool thing is that these people are all around you. They embody those characteristics like confidence, assertiveness and willingness to listen without judgement.

The Missing Piece in Self-Love

In many years of research, client interaction and experience, I have found one piece of significant evidence that resilience is indeed possible. The voices of those who have overcome adversity speak loudly, declaring that ultimately resilience is a process of connection to people who've overcome similar struggles.

Step Two. Tell Your Story

Even though you have your story on continuous playback loop, running audibly 24/7 in your head, there is power and resilience in sharing it with someone. Remember Step 1: *Find Someone Resilient To Connect With*. When you do, that person will inevitably share his/her story with you. She will offer evidence by sharing her own struggles with you and how she was able to overcome them. There is so much power in discovering that you are not alone.

Far too many people feel alone in their struggles. At my retreats, the participants cling tightly to their shame, not wanting to expose it. Yet by the end of the first few hours, each of them shares openly, albeit selectively, to other participants. It is beautiful to witness.

Humans crave connection. Yet, our fears, such as rejection, silence us. It is only when one person speaks up, sharing his or her own inadequacies, which allow us to consider sharing our own. Time lines and events may be different, but the color of pain is the same. It is dark and it is ugly and it pierces our core.

By telling people about the experience which led you to feel shame, you are making a direct connection between the events that led to your shame and the people who are there to help you through it by listening to you. By coming together with people who will listen without judging, you'll be cutting shame out of the picture, weakening its power over you until you eventually let go of it completely and you're able to tell your story without shame.

In my trainings I am very forward, very open. I share vulnerably the pain I have experienced. I also share the hope and possibility that I felt when I first began to share and connect. I began to feel alive again when I found yet another woman who had overcome violence. I was no longer alone. Neither are you. There are countless resources available for you. Our world is beginning to shift into one of support and possibility. The stigma of asking for help is diminishing. One of the coolest and most precious gifts I've received is to meet thousands of powerful women and men who have overcome a significant life crisis and are now supporting those still struggling.

The hardest part is taking that very first step towards breaking your silence. It's hard to let go of old beliefs you've held onto for so long. However, the other side of shame is a way of living filled with self-love. Can you even imagine?

I have come down a long road to be here. I don't feel the shame I used to feel, but I know I'm exposing a very important part of my life when I share.

Embracing your own vulnerability is never easy- it still makes me uncomfortable to share my story, because it represents a version of me that is so unfamiliar. Yet, I know that short-term discomfort has led me to long-term healing. Another way to define resilience: the ability to keep on challenging yourself, resulting in an ever-increasing personal strength.

That's the very reason I share in all my workshops. Each time I put myself out there and expose what happened to me, I know that the memory has less power over me. It will always be there but it won't always have power over me as I become more resilient.

Another reason I share is because the healing process is never quite finished, even for me. This is not to discourage or overwhelm you but simply to show that although life is about to get much better for you once you unload your shame and share your story, there's still a challenge ahead.

This is a challenge I welcome with open arms, though. It's a *good* challenge, one which makes me better, stronger, more positive. It's nothing compared to the impossible challenge of keeping my shame a secret.

So yes, sharing your story may be challenging at first. But soon you'll simply be concerned with the challenges that make you stronger as you learn to share your story and start whittling away at the shame that used to grow inside of you. *That's* resilience.

Finally, I wholeheartedly believe that when we dare to risk and share with those seeking help, from a place of understanding and empathy, we can create a lasting impact. One of the first moments of vulnerability include me stating that I am not an expert. I am no better than anyone that I work with. I'm just a little further down the road. I have a solid footing, and I'm willing to hold out my hand. I implore you to find someone who is willing to listen.

One of the biggest hurdles to overcome in the beginning of making changes is to tell your story of where you are and how you're really feeling. Once you do, it is as if there is a hundred pound weight lifted off your chest. And then the real work begins. I hope that I'm not scaring you too much. I know the road to self-love seems like an endless and impossible mountain. I also know that the view from the other side, just over the ridge - is spectacular. And you my dear, are worth it!

Compiled By Kate Gardner

Sylvia Friedman

For over 25 years, Sylvia Friedman has been changing people's lives - one TRUTH at a time.

As a motivational speaker, intuitive coach, handwriting analyst, astrologer and celebrated author, she not only sees the truth in others, she helps them discover it themselves. From the hallways of neighborhood housing projects, to the boardrooms of Chicago's top companies, to college classrooms and entertainment venues all around the world, Sylvia has guided individuals from all walks of life on a journey of self-awareness and acceptance with her signature blend of comedy, candor and compassion.

A graduate of Northwestern University's journalism and theatre programs, Sylvia has been featured on many media outlets, including *Oprah*, *Donohue*, *190 North*, Lifetime, Fox, WGN, WLS and WJBC.

She is a recent recipient of an Inspired Award from *Today's Chicago Woman* magazine, and her book, **The Stars in Your Family: Relationships between Parents and Children** (Hay House), is in its 5th printing.

The Missing Piece in Self-Love

Visit Sylvia's website at www.sylviafriedman.com to view client comments and read how Sylvia has helped others find the TRUTH.

For private consultations, to schedule a workshop, entertainment or engage a powerful speaker/guest, contact Sylvia at 312-944-7256.

Compiled By Kate Gardner

We Must Not Only Educate the Mind, But Also the Heart

By Sylvia Friedman

WE MUST NOT ONLY EDUCATE THE MIND, BUT ALSO THE HEART. Kobi Yamada

My father asked me this question when I was 7 years old. He said, "Baby, what makes you happy?"

I smiled and said, "Daddy, love is the answer." He laughed out loud, as he usually did, and said, "I'm going to tell the whole family that my baby girl needs a lot of love."

I'm so grateful to have had the courage and support of my loving father, when I needed to recognize and understand my talents and ability. As I grew up and changed my careers, I always think of daddy. I lost him early, but I always speak to him and say, "Daddy keep believing in me!"

My parents were immigrants. My mother did not know how to read and write, and daddy had a ninth grade education. Daddy was a wise man and provided all of the tools I needed to develop self-love. Mama was a very frightened woman, and did not have a clue on how to raise me. I am an only child and my mother could not understand how to discipline me. I was feisty and bright and that was very frustrating to her. She had to think of a way to get me to obey her. Her way of making me understand that I was a bad girl was to pretend to faint. She would faint on a chair, the couch, the bed, the floor—anywhere, in order to scare me. The

The Missing Piece in Self-Love

first time it happened I was four years old. I was playing with my only doll, Bessie when Mama collapsed on the chair.

I ran over to see what was wrong and she barely lifted her head saying that I was a bad girl, and I made her faint. I ran to the kitchen cabinet and got a glass. I poured some water and brought it to her. Mama began to do this very often until I decided that she was going to STOP. I said to Bessie, my soulmate, that mama was fooling me and I was going to tell her. I walked over to my mother and said, "I'm not going to bring you any more water, and I'm not a bad girl. You are tricking me!

Somehow I knew that if I had listened to my mother she would turn my self-love into extreme insecurity. My father saved me by complimenting me all the time. You are special, you are beautiful, and you are so smart. Of course I chose to believe him.

I spent the first twelve years of my life living in the Chicago Housing Projects on Roosevelt Road. Our particular building was just built when we moved in, but it was surrounded by what people referred to as the ghetto. We were a poor family, but somehow I never felt poor. My father would say that I was born positive and happy, with a strong zest for life. I guess that I'm still like that.

Daddy did not realize that his unconditional love was the tool for my early stage of self-love. Diversity was all around me on a daily basis, since the housing projects were filled with African Americans, Hispanics, Jews, Italians, Greeks, and what my little Jewish grandma called 'billhillies'. I thank God that I was born with psychic ability and innate courage. I believe that these gifts were the keys to believing in myself and developing self-love. I always believed that I was responsible to take care of my little friends. Their parents were mostly alcoholics, prostitutes, and many had been in prison. I felt that I was so lucky to have my father. My friends did not receive a lot of love, so most of our games included love, hugging, kissing, and fun parties at my house.

This project story, one of many, deeply marked me. I was only eight when it happened. My girlfriend Barbara was my best friend. She was only six, but I was drawn to protect her. I saved her from being raped by her father. Barbara was a sweet and gentle child, but her fear of life and her father was monumental. She looked like my doll Bessie, who had soft curly blonde hair, big blue eyes, and a beautiful heart shaped mouth. Barbara and Bessie were my best friends.

Barbara would cry a lot, and I needed to ask her, "Why do you cry so much?" She finally told me that her father, Jack, was hurting her. I asked, "What do you mean hurting you?" She touched her vagina and said, "My daddy is putting his peepee inside of me. She was six years old and did not fully comprehend what was happening to her.

I don't know how I understood, but I did. Her mother Rose was a nice woman, but oblivious to what was happening to her daughter. She did not want to know that her husband, who was an alcoholic, would rape her daughter.

One day Barbara was crying so bitterly I said, "I'm going to tell your mother!" She started to scream, "PLEASE DON'T TELL MY MOTHER!" Of course I didn't listen to her and want into the kitchen to speak to her mother. I said, "Rose, Jack is raping Barbara." She got angry and said, "What are you talking about?" I got angry and said, "I know what a penis is, my daddy told me." I must admit that I was embarrassed, but I was not going to stop. As we were talking, Jack was coming in the back door. I ran into Barbara's room and peeked through the door. I saw Rose stare at Jack and she was accusing him of raping Barbara. He crossed over

The Missing Piece in Self-Love

to grab her when she put her hand in the drawer and grabbed a small gun. I thought I was in a movie when she shot at him. She missed and shot again. Fortunately, she missed and told him to pack his clothes and get out. He said, "Why do you believe Sylvia?" She responded with "because she does not lie."

I never saw Jack again. Rose thanked me and said, "You have a special gift. Thank you for saving your best friend." Barbara stayed my friend until she was 28. As she died in my arms from ulcerated colitis, I hugged and kissed her goodbye. My face was so wet, because I couldn't stop the tears!

My self-love was my protection. I got through so many situations because of it, and I needed others to love themselves. As I grew up no one abused me. No one had the right to take their violence out on me.

My life in the housing projects taught me the deep importance of self-love. I was so grateful that my pain was minimal next to the suffering of my friends. Hearing my father say that our life was beautiful compared to the life of people lying in the middle of the street. I looked at him and said, "God bless you daddy.

I graduated from grammar school at almost 12 years old. They skipped me three times because I excelled in my learning. It was not a good thing for a 12 year old, who was 20 lbs overweight to enter high school chubby and two years younger than everyone else. Because of my parents lack of education they thought that I was brilliant. I was 20 lbs overweight, and tried very hard to lose those extra pounds. I did and I was not embarrassed to enter high school. My only dream was to be an actress and get a standing ovation. I graduated high school at almost 16 and got into Northwestern University. I graduated with a degree in speech, drama, and journalism.

After graduation I went to New York with my best friend. I was going to be an actress and she was going to find a husband. She found three. I started to audition and was doing well when I met my husband. I did not want to get married but he was the one to bring me my two outstanding children. I raised my children with my philosophy "Love is the answer". They are my greatest accomplishments.

My husband was not for me and since I am psychic I knew that. We divorced after 10 years and I went back to acting. I met the love of my life, and our relationship lasted 12 years. We acted, directed, wrote scripts and loved each other deeply. Unfortunately, his soon to be ex-wife started to commit suicide to stop him from marrying me. He cried and said "I must go back home." I was in shock and responded with, "I will never speak to you again" and, I didn't. My father died three days later and now I had lost the two loves of my life. My self-love saved me from losing my mind and my children were there all the way.

I built many careers, acting 10 years on the stage, producing 7 years and development director for The Heart Association 8 years. I have been in my own business for over 15 years. I am a life coach that teaches self-love and I am a motivational speaker and published author of, THE STARS IN YOUR FAMILY, raising your kids as to who they are, rather than who you expect them to be. The book has been very successful and many people call it their bible. I am so pleased to have a chapter in this book because self-love saved my life.

I have changed the life of many people and very proud that I had the ability to help them. I believe that I practice what I preach. I have so much more to say, but my next book Truthful Love will tell you much more.

The Missing Piece in Self-Love

So many human beings search for what they call "true love" and I tell them that finding self-love will bring them a much happier life as they live their truth. I want to thank my outstanding father and the housing projects for teaching me the value of Self-love.

Compiled By Kate Gardner

Toni Idiaquez

Toni Idiaquez is an International Best-Selling Author, PNI Business Coach and Founder of New Life 360.

As a PNI Business Coach, Toni discovers the root cause of why you are where you are in your business, clears the root cause and provides you with practical business tools for you to implement so you can succeed.

Toni guidance is compassionate and the mind-set tools she gives you help you become empowered and self-confident everywhere in your life.

Toni's goal is to help you thrive in your business and your life where it causes a positive ripple effect in the world.

You can reach Toni at:

Website:
www.newlife360.com

The Missing Piece in Self-Love

Self-Love – Selflessly Selfish
By Toni Idiaquez

For the past 30 years I have been on a journey to have Self-love, although I didn't know that is what I was doing. I thought I was trying to get over the death of my Father and how to deal with that death.

Due to the death of my father when I was a teenager, I operated from a belief that I had to give up myself in order to be loved.

This unconscious belief was anything but loving to me, it was detrimental to my well-being on every level of my Being! These beliefs came from my interpretation of my father's death and the environment that I found myself in. I eventually put everyone first, my family, my friends, my ex-husband(s), lovers, and clients. I became exhausted, angry and resentful! Not a place that I truly wanted to live from....that place of invisible bondage, emotional pain, being the walking dead.

Through my search to heal my emotional wounds I found a very wise teacher who told me to let go of all of my unloving feelings, the ones that caused me pain. So, I set about doing that and the more unloving feelings I let go of the lighter I felt. I had to look deep within at the unloving feelings I had not only for others but also, for myself. Then I had to go deeper, look at and surrender the programs of my ancestors, those feelings of betrayal from their eyes that were running me! Once these programs were cleared, then and only then, I came to love myself and others, without attachment or expectations inherited from my ancestors and the accumulation from my experience of life. Ever hear of "Sins of the father" or "Seven generational curse".

The best example of love without attachments and expectations I observed were in animals and I will use dogs as an example. I believe that most would agree the unconditional love a dog brings! Dogs are happy to see you, even if you leave just for a minute then come back they jump for joy, wagging their tails and giving wet kisses! Dogs know when you need their love, they come closer when you are sad or crying or just don't feel good. An animal's love is pure, without expectation. Why do you think they can do this? Dogs don't self-talk….you're stupid, or ugly, etc.…. they are just being dogs the way Spirit created them.

What I found that was the most harmful to me was not having strong clear boundaries. No wasn't a no! Especially when it came to my husband(s) or partner in life. I discovered I had a belief that my father died because when I stood up for myself and I said no to him, he died and the love went away, i.e. I have to give myself away or love goes away. This wasn't a conscious thought but one that got stuck in my belief system when I was in shock over his death. I found myself in unhealthy relationships, where I wasn't honoured or respected because I didn't honour and respect myself and my Spirit was dying. I decided that I wanted my freedom from my past more than I wanted my current unhealthy relationship. This was the hardest decision I had ever made because I loved this man, I still do. So, I kept my word and I let go of the belief that I had to give myself up to be loved and the relationship ended. When I made a clear boundary, he disconnected, events happened which ended the relationship, and I moved out. I am so glad I did, as it was the craziest making environment I had ever been in.

The Missing Piece in Self-Love

I also discovered that I made the best out of what I found myself in. This pattern stemmed from making the best out of life given the circumstances of my father's death. What I finally discovered was that I had a choice. I didn't even realize I was operating as if I didn't. So a question I ask myself on a regular basis is "Is this good for my own well-being"? If it's yes and I want to do it, then I do it. If it isn't in the best interest of my wellbeing then I don't.

Now, I choose healthy relationships with people who are kind, respectful, supportive, loving and easy to be around. People who stand on their own and don't suck the life out of someone. I made a decision to identify deal breakers and to not go against them because if I did it would be painful for all parties involved, and it is truly the most loving thing to do.

Another way I choose to love myself is to eat healthy, drink clean water and exercise. This looks like balanced eating where I feel good. Food must taste good, no cardboard tasting food but homemade with love is my all-time favorite. If it doesn't taste good forget it…life is too short! My body loves to move, I feel good during and after working out. Exercise releases feel good endorphins plus there are so many rewards from health to feeling sexy and every aspect in between. On occasion, I eat desert first! Simply for the fun of it without excuses! It's fun, and you should try it. One of my all-time favorites is cheesecake, and I make a great cheesecake! My body is the Temple my spirit resides in and why not make it a glorious temple.

Speaking about taking care of the temple, I express self-love by taking care of my health by resting when tired, soaking in a hot bath with essential oils, getting massages, chiropractic care, and acupuncture on a regular basis or when needed.

I laugh a lot! I mean deep belly laughs where my cheeks and stomach hurts! In fact I have a rule in my office…its laughter! You know the saying "Laughter does us good like medicine". On many occasions my best friend and I become real silly, punch drunk silly when we have conversations, it relieves the stress and seriousness of our lives. This all started in school when we would stay up late studying for exams, now it can be first thing in the morning. I usually end up with an aching belly, mascara running down my face and a lighter feeling in my spirit.

Another one of my most favorite things to do is dance! From silly to sensual, especially belly dance. One of my favorite memories of dancing growing up is my father teaching me how to dance. He would have me put my feet on his and we would waltz. Still to this day anytime music is playing my body moves.

Spend time in nature is being with Spirit! The awe I feel while being amongst the mountains in Georgia or the Rocky Mountains, both so different yet inspiring! I have two absolute favorite times of the day… sunrise and sun set! The stillness in the morning with the sun is rising. I have to say that Colorado has my favorite sunrises with purple, bluish grey and orange in the sky its just breath taking! My favorite sunsets are in Arizona – orange, yellows and reds so vibrant it takes my breath away. I call these times of take painted skies with Spirit being the artist.

Alone time with Spirit in prayer! Nothing feels so nourishing to my spirit and soul as fasting prayer for me! My two favorite ways are when I am on Hanblecea (Vision Quest) and Sun Dance Ceremony. The oneness I feel when Spirit talks to me through feeling, words, dreams, and visions, I know I am wrapped in the arms of the Divine! Other ways I spend alone time with Spirit is meditation – my mind becomes quiet and I expand in awareness of self and Spirit, the unbreakable connection. By taking time to be with the Divine in me and the Divine that is everywhere, that

The Missing Piece in Self-Love

created this earth and all of us is pure bliss and fills me up more than food itself.

One of my favorite ways that I love myself is that I take vacations that are simply vacations! What I have noticed is that my vacations were always tied into either work or ceremonies. I would feel guilty if I was just having fun. Besides that in the past it always became about the question am I putting this money to good use as I wanted to be a good steward.

I look in the mirror and tell myself "I love you" and I do! There was a time when I couldn't even look myself in the eye. Now, I give myself a love bath on a regular basis.

What I have noticed that when I take care of myself, I have self-acceptance, I love myself and I have more joy when helping others. My life is about service to others in joy and love.

Compiled By Kate Gardner

Violeta Rajacic

Violeta Rajacic earned a diploma in Business Management. For the past ten years she has been stay-at-home parent. She volunteered for a local Food Bank, Outreach for a local Street Church and does Crisis Peer-Mentoring. Four years ago when a tragic event shattered her world, leaving her a single mom, she realized it was time to take inventory and examine every broken piece of her heart and soul. Feeling unloved and abandoned in the worst possible way, she discovered what God's love for her is, which led her onto the path of finding that "missing piece". This is her story…

You can reach Violeta at:

Facebook:
Violeta Rajacic

Email:
violeta_rajacic@live.ca

The Missing Piece in Self-Love

Filling Up on God's Love
By Violeta Rajacic

My understanding of love was pretty simple and it was like anything else in life: you had to deserve to be loved. It was not my birth right. At least, that's what I was told all of my life. The amount of love I would receive from others was directly proportionate to what I would do, or not do for them… and vice versa.

I kept walking through life without ever looking inside of me, but always looking on the outside for that love, acceptance, and approval. So I learned how to fill my love tank whenever it would start running on empty; through relationships, partying, constantly being surrounded by company (that wasn't always for my highest good), acquiring material things, to name a few methods. The tank would run empty as soon as I filled it up, as if it had a leak I could not permanently fix.

The more I tried to keep things under control, the more they kept spinning out of control. Simply put, I could not escape from feeling unloved, no matter how hard I tried. It never really dawned on me how screwed up I was until that horrific day in July of 2011, when I got my wake-up call. The love of my life and father of our son, took his own life just two days before our son's 6th birthday.

My heart and soul shattered. Every feeling I was trying so hard to escape from all of my life, washed over me, enveloping me into this nauseating whirlpool of despair. I hit rock bottom in the ocean of my emotions. While I was drowning in guilt, shame, abandonment, rejection, self-loathing and condemnation, huge waves of anger and rage lifted me up from the bottom and tossed me wildly onto the rocky shore of grief. I survived the shipwreck of my own life, however, broken into thousand little pieces.

They say death is a great teacher. It sure showed me that everything I used to cling to could be wiped out in one fell swoop and there was absolutely nothing I could do about it. The mask fell off and I was forced to examine every broken piece of myself.

For the first month I had my best friend stay with my son and me. That weekend she was supposed to be moving 600 miles away, but she stayed and took care of us. I don't remember much from that period. Finally, she had to leave and for the next seven months, I found myself basically alone. I had one other girl friend that would come around and check on us. My ailing mother lives in Europe, and her health and finances would not allow for her to come here and be by my side.

All the other "friends" I thought I had disappeared as if I had some horrible, infectious disease. I didn't know that's what my grief looked like on the outside. People just didn't know what to say to me and how to handle me being broken. Until then, I was the pillar of strength and a person of support they would run to when their life was falling apart. Now I was someone who needed support. It became very clear to me that all of those "friendships" were a one-way streets and I had to re-evaluate that part of my life too. For the longest time, all I felt was anger.

I could not comprehend Jerry's actions; I could not understand why his family was stonewalling me, and why my friends weren't there for me? For goodness sake, we had a child together that he loved and cherished more than anything in this world! How could he do this to him?? Never mind me! I cried for six months straight. I would take our son to school, come home, and cry all day until I had to pick him up again. I couldn't let our son see me like that, so I held it together in front of him. As soon as I was out of his sight, tears came like flood. I seriously didn't think I would ever be able to stop crying. I would clutch The Bible to my chest and rock back and forth screaming silently inside. The slew of "whys" would never be answered; he did not leave a suicide note. I did not know how to get past that. The grief of suicide is a totally different ball game than any other grieving process I had endured throughout my life, and I had my fair share.

I started going to grief counselling to be able to make some sense out of a totally senseless situation. My grief counsellor was an older gentlemen and I happened to be his last client before he officially retired. God bless him. He kept me going for the time being and after he retired I did not seek a different counsellor. It only lasted six months; however, I was grateful for the time he spent listening to me. His support helped me focus on what I was able to do instead of what I couldn't do.

After he retired, that awful feeling of being alone and abandoned resurfaced again, but this time I took it straight to God. I started journaling "my conversations" with the Lord and I asked Him to take my pain away. After what I thought were unanswered prayers, I realised I was not giving Him what I was asking Him to take away. I was holding onto that pain as the last piece of my shipwreck. Slowly, I started moving through the grieving process. As I was letting go, in little bits and pieces the Lord started showing me His love. It came through different people that started showing up in my life. I connected with Jerry's family and my circle of friends changed completely with only a few coming back from what I now call "my past life". I forgave their absence in my time of need and understood their inability to be my support network.

I started volunteering for a local Food Bank as a client intake associate which helped me in a tremendous way to start feeling good about myself. I had a purpose and I was doing something for the community at large. After about year and a half, I joined a local Street Church, was baptised as a Christian, and started volunteering for their Outreach program. That experience transformed my life completely. With that transformation, the concept of self-love took on a totally different dimension. I realised that the only alternative to loving myself was not to hate myself, as I had been, but to fully grasp and enjoy God's love for me. He loves me just the way he designed me; I don't have to do anything special to deserve His love. It is always there without condition. The outpouring of His blessings in my life has been enormous in many, many ways. I don't have a room in this chapter to list them all, and if I mention one, I have to mention them all. They know who they are.

Today, the emotional pain is no longer searing; however, I did develop physical symptoms of post trauma: I have fibromyalgia, IBS, and anxiety which can sometimes hit me out of nowhere.

I get a little squirrely about month and a half prior to anniversary of Jerry's passing, but I am aware of that, so I take extra special care of myself. I try not to engage in anything that takes my emotional energy and I am kind to myself. Birthdays are still little hard time for me. As I already mentioned, he passed away two days before our son's birthday, but he was also cremated a day before my birthday.

This year, however, we both had wonderful birthdays and were showered with love from friends and family. I thank God for that. We are slowly moving upward and onward.

Nowadays, alone time is my time with God and I make sure there is plenty of it. Solitude is something I crave because crowds are emotionally draining for me after a while. What used to fill me before is what I stay away from now, and what I thought would never fill me is what fills me up now. My love tank is always full and overflowing, and I give my love without expecting anything in return: through a hug, a kind word to a stranger, an encouragement, a prayer, and little things like that. I still mentor others in their times of crisis and I would encourage everyone to surrender any obstacle to Him in your time of trouble and He will bring you through it. You are His Beloved child.

"Trust in the Lord with all your heart and do not lean on your own understanding"
Proverbs 3:5

Compiled By Kate Gardner

Virin Gomber

Virin Gomber is a Success Coach, Motivational Speaker, Thought Innovator and Author who empowers businesses and individuals to achieve successful breakthroughs and balance, professionally and personally.

He specialises in helping small to medium business enterprises, especially women entrepreneurs and professionals, to leverage their inner resources and realize their full potential in order to achieve their goals much faster.

Virin is passionate about consistent and ongoing growth in all areas of life – health, career, wealth, relationships, spirituality and learning. His mission is to make a positive difference through empowering people with solution-focused skills and mindset excellence.

When speaking to an audience, Virin inspires, motivates, galvanizes and propels people into taking immediate action towards their goals, utilizing a holistic approach.

With an enthusiasm for personal growth and a strong understanding of various forms of success modalities, Virin is dedicated to transforming lives globally for his vision of collective growth.

You're invited to connect with Virin at:

Website:
www.viringomber.com

Website:
www.mindfulsolutions.co.nz

Compiled By Kate Gardner

Unravelling Your Real Self
By Virin Gomber

As I drove towards the gym for my regular workout, I felt a weird sensation – a strange mix of discomfort, excitement, enthusiasm, uncertainty and calm – all at the same time. The sensation also felt familiar in some ways, further adding to the weirdness of this experience.

I ignored it all, wondering if I had something strange to eat for lunch or if I was drinking too much coffee.

At the gym, half way into my workout, as I stopped to look into one of the hundreds of mirrors around me, the sensation suddenly came back. This time it was completely overwhelming.

I experienced an immense surge of self-love!

In that moment, I sensed a huge appreciation for who I was and how life had turned out for me. I felt deeply grateful for all the abundance in my life – robust health, affluence, nurturing family, loving friends, and all the small and big incidents that led me to where I was.

And then something else happened that I wasn't expecting at all - my eyes welled up with tears! Tears of intense gratitude!

Strangely enough, I got out of that feeling without me even trying. That's when my conscious mind took over and started evaluating this incredible moment.

Since childhood, I have had experiences when I connected with myself. But, this was the first time it revolved around self-love.

The Missing Piece in Self-Love

Skinny years

As a child, I used to be a skinny and shy kid. I was physically smaller compared to most of my peers. And when I say shy, I mean 'terribly introverted'. I would dread initiating anything in any situation. I was a follower and enjoyed the comfort of doing things I was told to do.

Being an introvert, I had a limited number of friends. I never communicated freely, clearly and comprehensively in most situations. This resulted in people around me, including my family and friends, misunderstanding me.

I always wanted to hide myself from the eyes of the world. This was a result of, and also further contributed to, some kids picking on me. To my understanding, they were jealous because I was academically bright despite my size.

Though a bright student, I was never a topper at school – always finishing at second or third spot.

Growing up, I also discovered that I had quite a non-traditional way of thinking. I was an 'outside the box' kid. I would question the traditional ways of life. This, coupled with the fact I wasn't communicating clearly about my thoughts, started causing friction in my relationships with my family as well as with myself.

While I don't particularly remember any moments from my childhood when I really appreciated who I was, I do remember occasionally being thankful for a nurturing family, especially my parents, and more especially my mother. I was always quite close to my two siblings, both brothers.

But it wasn't sufficient enough to help me break free of my introverted mental barriers.

Terrible teens - years of upheaval

My personal challenges started to grow when I entered my teens. I began to feel more misunderstood by my family and peers.

As a growing teenager, I became more strongly opinionated. While I would generally try to follow some of my parents' instructions aimed at aligning with the societal norms, I was turning more rebellious and withdrawn.

I would wonder why we were supposed to live our life a certain way in order to please our relatives, our neighbours and the society around us. I questioned why saying my mind when responding to my 'elders' would be considered a disrespectful gesture.

All this added to the existing conflicts and made me feel isolated. I started doubting myself, thinking if I was right at all the way I was.

My inner critic started controlling my life and a sense of self-hate became my constant companion. I felt vulnerable, as a variety of fears started to grip my psyche.

Young adult: Fight, Flight or Freeze?

These thought patterns continued to build a disempowering belief system inside of me, making me feel insufficient as a human being. This grew stronger as I became a young adult. I started craving for some magical healing that could cure my lack of worth.

And then, I happened to meet a girl who, I felt, understood the real me.

Being classmates at a language institute, we got to see each other regularly. I started developing a strong liking for her as I

The Missing Piece in Self-Love

respected her views as much as she respected mine. Before I knew, I found myself deeply in love with her. I began to regain my sense of worthiness.

However, being shy, I never had the courage to express my love.

In the following months, I started sensing something wasn't right about my understanding of this feeling of love I was carrying. I was getting confused about the lack of reciprocity of my feelings for her.

The bombshell dropped when one day I got to know she was leaving the country to settle overseas and get married!

I was devastated… heartbroken… destroyed. I felt rejected and worthless… again. The feelings of disillusion, insufficiency and lack of worth engulfed me again. My confidence disappeared into oblivion.

Obviously I had completely misunderstood her friendship for love.

Consequently, any remaining faith I had in myself and my abilities vanished. I started indulging in hateful self-talk. The rejection made me reject myself.

I felt like locking up my story of rejection with a big fat lock and running away from it all.

But there was something that kept me going, and perhaps dimly hopeful about my life. It was my family's loving support. While I still felt misunderstood at many levels, there was this unbreakable and profound bonding with them that helped me gradually pick up the shattered pieces of my emotional self.

Making sense of self

Flash-forward 15 years.

Compiled By Kate Gardner

Having been in a total rut and deep in a trough for so many years, I realized I had nothing more to lose.

Over this period, I found myself studying various personal development modalities and learning from a range of inspirational leaders. I found that most of these motivators had a story of their own… a story that may have sounded unique but had stark similarities with my story and thousands of other human stories. Most of these people had experienced a variety of life challenges, including - poverty, hunger, depression, insufficient love, domestic violence, emotional rollercoasters and lack of self-worth.

I was amazed to discover how some of these people had turned their life around, utilizing their resolve and determination, to the level where they were now assisting others achieve the same.

I got to learn the science of how our brain operates and how we can change our results in life by changing some of our habits and patterns of thoughts.

Regular and dedicated practice of imprinting new thought patterns into my mind gradually started to change the way I thought of myself. I saw and experienced a new emergence of my own being.

While this new journey wasn't easy for me, it was worth the tremendous effort I put into it. Occasionally, I would find myself slipping back into my old 'self-hate' mode. But I was now operating with a strong and solid determination to unravel a new Virin, which I realized was my real self and the one who was desperately waiting to be unveiled.

This process of self-sculpting included connecting with my inner being, facing my hidden fears and observing the dark crevices deep within me – even while ensuring it didn't pull me back down

The Missing Piece in Self-Love

into those negative loops. It also involved embracing new ways of thinking to propel me toward a state where I started to appreciate my being, respect my life, accept myself as I was and love every bit of my existence.

This was incredibly life-changing for me!

I couldn't have imagined, back then when I was a skinny little boy, that one day I would morph into a success coach helping individuals to become their best selves and live extraordinary lives. It's nothing less than magical that today I'm involved in coaching individuals and businesses to transform their professional and personal lives through unleashing their own hidden powers. I've become more of an active leader, rather than a passive follower that I used to be.

As I do this, I find it immensely rewarding to be able to inspire thousands of people to begin connecting with themselves and igniting their self-love so they can unveil the abundant being within and also help others around them to do so.

Loving yourselves can be one of the most challenging things because oftentimes you feel the need for an external endorsement to make you feel good about yourselves.

As soon as you change that belief to the one where you start accepting yourself and feel completely self-sufficient, that's when loving yourself becomes much easier. This powerful mind-set eventually elevates you to levels of higher consciousness, abundance and happiness.

"Love is misunderstood to be an emotion; actually, it is a state of awareness, a way of being in the world, a way of seeing oneself and others."

Dr. David Hawkins

Compiled By Kate Gardner

Yvette Mason

Yvette Mason is an Author, Artist and Motivational Coach.

She often tells people "I travel the Internet, leaving sprinkles of happiness wherever I go".

Yvette writes books on motivation, weight loss and self-love. As an artist, she is launching a new line of products titled "Intentionally Yours: Where intentions become art". She also does original works on canvas, stone and jewelry.

As a Motivational Coach, her motto is "Helping others to become the best version of themselves – Mind Body & Spirit". She has traveled the US as an International Trainer and has taught classes at a Technical College.

You can reach Yvette at:

Website:
www.coachyvette.com

The "Lost Puppy" Syndrome
By Yvette Mason

Ever since I was a little girl, I have had a love for animals. I cannot ever remember a time when they were not present within my life. Their vulnerability and need for love enchanted me. In fact, the needier they were, the more I was drawn to them. A lost puppy was not lost for long! They were quickly given a home, love and attention. I made it my mission to fix those poor souls. I did this not only for the love of them, but also for the love I received in return. I felt a sense of accomplishment by providing help. This trend stayed with me throughout my adult years.

I am 50 years young – times were much different then. When I was a child, I grew up to watching "I Dream of Jeanie" and "Bewitched". I would fantasize about being magic myself, being able to alter my surroundings and escaping into a dreamland that was perfect. I also grew up in a time when drug usage and alcoholism was not viewed the same as it is today. It was a recreational pastime, enjoyed by many, often in public! Television commercials would glamorize men and women drinking, even on commercials. Housewives would saunter across the room with a highball. It is no wonder why so many people became addicted. Unfortunately, my unsuspecting parents were also part of that crowd. One moment they were doing it recreationally and the next moment, it had seized control of their lives. When the addiction monster took control over their senses, I would practice my magic and take a journey to that dreamland…

Before I started to practice "magic", my mother was a very beautiful, elegant woman. I remember wanting to do everything with her, talking about anything I wanted to. I would lie in bed next to her, just listening to her wisdom. My father worked hard to provide us a lifestyle that I felt was glamorous. My mother and I would have our hair done the same, wear matching furs and even similar jewelry. I had a diamond tiara that Cinderella herself would have envied. I was a princess, and my mother was the queen.

Slowly, things started to change. She became distant from my father and me. She would sleep during the day, which was not like her. The house started to become messy, more so day by day. The beautiful woman started to look ashen. Her appearance was no longer elegant. The cherished mother and daughter talks were becoming less frequent, eventually whittling down to none. I did my best to try and please her, hoping to bring her back. When my brother was born, I was 5 years old. While my mother slept, I would take care of him. I would quiet him, feed him, change his diaper and provide him company. It became a secret that my mother and I kept private. Somehow, she would pull it together enough by the time my father would arrive home, avoiding suspicion of something amiss.

Then she started leaving during the day. In her defence, she did ensure that I was cared for and watched. Unfortunately, my babysitter was a 17 year old boy who did not have my wellbeing in his mind. What he did have in his mind was having sex with this 8 year old. He was not stupid; he took his time to earn my trust. He would talk about how my parents loved each other. He would ask me if I wanted that type of love. He seduced me into believing that what we had *was* love, and what he was wanted to do with me was *not* wrong. He brainwashed me by telling me that people in love do those types of things. It was just a natural, beautiful thing. I believed him. I was lonely and missing my mother. I didn't have any friends. I had become a little heavier

The Missing Piece in Self-Love

and children would pick on me. So, I gave in after much persistence. Even though a small part of my little mind thought something was not right, he would quickly reassure me that it *was* right. He told me not to tell my parents, or my love would be taken away.

My mother started to spiral downwards. She had found a new love: heroin. At 8 years old, I knew how to "shoot up". I didn't quite understand what she was doing, but I will never forget seeing her do it. I would watch her go through the motions of the process and then watch her drift away into a coma-like silence. I was fortunate to have my babysitter – he provided me the company and love that she had taken away from me.

My father then became suspicious of her doings and things got worse. Fighting became a daily event. My father took on the duties of the housewife, taking care of the house when he could. He was trying the best he could, for a woman that he deeply loved. All the effort he gave could not keep her home. Sometimes she would drag me along to "score". While she ran out with a pimp to find her drugs, his prostitute would babysit me. I will say that the pimp and prostitute were kind souls. Ironically, they treated me much better than the babysitter…

One day, it came to a head. My parents had fought terribly and she ran out. As I ran out after her, begging her to take me with her, she refused. She told me to go back inside and to take care of my father. She took off in a car, leaving this 9 year child on the side of the road. I watched her drive away sobbing. She never looked back. While I broke down badly, my father broke down worse. We were sent to live with my grandparents for a few of years, while my father tried to recover.

My grandmother doted over me and my brother. She would do everything in her power to make us happy. She took over the role of my missing mother in every way she could. When my father got his head back together, he soon met my now mother. My grandmother always stayed close in my life, me being the daughter she had never had.

I did finally confess what had happened with the babysitter when I was 13. My father was devastated. The boy had moved and I just wanted it all to go back away, so he dropped the issue. I grew up and moved on with my life, burying that secret deep inside of myself. I lost weight, got in great shape and one day met my now ex-husband.

Unfortunately, I gained weight after my first child. I finally dropped back down a few years later, only to get pregnant again. I gained 80 pounds and started to experience severe back and pelvic pain. In fact, it was extremely painful during intercourse. It caused a huge strain on our relationship. When I had my third and final child, I was heavy. While I did take care of my appearance to my best ability, my husband was no longer attracted to me. The more he would push me to diet, the more I escaped within food. It became my crutch, and soon my addiction. I would swing from binge eating to just constant eating. I left my husband when he said he was embarrassed by my looks and ashamed of me.

I have had various other semi-long term relationships since my ex-husband. Each one of the relationships drained me and helped them. The first suffered from bi-polar disease. I stayed with him for almost 6 years. While he was not an alcoholic, he did abuse pain pills. His manic swings became too much and I left. My next partner was much younger than myself and was very attractive. As an added bonus, he was a very functional drunk! We stuck it out for 5 years, but after my middle child became diagnosed with Cancer, we drifted apart. Next up was my married man partner.

The Missing Piece in Self-Love

Although he was separated and lived with my children and me, it never felt right with him not being legally divorced. He too was a very functional alcoholic and was even well loved in the community. Unfortunately, I invested a lot of my heart and he was investing his penis in other women.

Finally, in stepped my recent ex-partner. I remember the first moment I saw his ocean blue eyes. We had met when I was not single and had become friends. When he asked me to date him, I was excited, because this was the first man I was friends with first! We remained friends throughout the entire relationship and I thought we would one day be married. In *every other relationship*, I would be thin starting out, and would gain weight over time. This time I actually started out heavy and lost weight while *with* him! I lost 80 pounds and still have kept it off.

Sadly, he lost his job and drank all day. He was a happy drunk, but also a child when it came to responsibility. I paid for everything, supported his drinking and smoking habit, became his crutch and found myself heavily in debt. I started meditating, practicing self-love, working hard on self-improvement. Despite my best efforts, the strain had become so bad that I awoke one day and wanted to die.

Enter this book project. I was so excited to write about self-love! The stress was forgotten for a moment. I could share my weight-loss, meditation, self-love journey and help others! Then I realized, I couldn't truly say that I loved myself and stay in this relationship.

Since then, I have completely changed. I no longer recognize that old self. I meditate, do art, write, enjoy my own company and am at *peace*. I practice gratitude daily. I went through the forgiveness process for my biological mother and my molester. I can truly say I just feel sorrow, with no anger! I even stopped watching regular television and enrolled in many classes. I take care of my body, my mind and my spirit. For the first time in my life, I am content being alone. I am *so* happy that my son is having a chemotherapy treatment as I type, and I only feel bliss.

The other day at work, we found a puppy. The poor thing looked so sad and lonely. Every fibre in my being wanted to bring it home, care for it, help it and love it. I didn't though. I am done repeating my lost puppy syndrome.

Conclusion

To be the one to help bring together all these amazing people in one place is truly an honour and a privilege for me. I knew that along my journey of self-hate to self-love I was not alone, and clearly by the people that stand with me in this book, I was indeed right.

The facts state that 1 in 3 people have low self-esteem and very low self-confidence, which means a heck of a low percentage of people on this planet really do love themselves! The saddest part is that all these people feel like they are alone and think it's only happening to them, when really their best friend, neighbour, sister and brothers feel exactly the same way.

Self-love is the hardest journey that we will have to take and it will mean many more hurdles to jump over on our future path. However a step each day, and little by little the growth of self-love turns into something huge. Just remember you can't get out of bed one morning and just all of a sudden love yourself! Self-love is something that needs work and attention each and every day.

It's like a muscle that is built over time to get stronger. It needs a daily workout to become bigger and have a better impact on not just your life, but everyone else's life too.

When I began to love myself more I learnt new limits of deeper understanding of love. This then impacted the friendships and relationships I had around me and helped them be more soul connected and be overall amazing to experience.

Compiled By Kate Gardner

I hope by the stories shared in this book that we touch your own life and make you realise you are worthy of love… Self-Love!

With Love & Appreciation

Kate Gardner

9 x Best-Selling Author/International Success Coach & CEO of The Missing Piece Publishing House.

www.themissingpiecepublishing.com

The Missing Piece in Self-Love

The Missing Piece
Publishing

Invites you to compile your very own book in the International Best-Selling Book Series. We pay YOU up to $3,000 to become a published author and have every intention of taking you to the best-sellers list, just like every other book in the series!

For more information please visit

www.themissingpublishing.com

Compiled By Kate Gardner

The is not the end, it's just the beginning ☺